MAKING
NEIGHBORHOODS
WHOLE

A Handbook for Christian Community Development

Wayne Gordon
& John M. Perkins
with Randall Frame

Foreword by Shane Claiborne

IVP Books

An imprint of InterVarsity Press
Downers Grove, Illinois

InterVarsity Press
P.O. Box 1400, Downers Grove, IL 60515-1426
ivpress.com
email@ivpress.com

InterVarsity Press® is the book-publishing division of InterVarsity Christian Fellowship/USA®, a movement of students and faculty active on campus at hundreds of universities, colleges and schools of nursing in the United States of America, and a member movement of the International Fellowship of Evangelical Students. For information about local and regional activities, visit intervarsity.org.

All Scripture quotations, unless otherwise indicated, are taken from THE HOLY BIBLE, NEW INTERNATIONAL VERSION®, NIV® Copyright © 1973, 1978, 1984, 2011 by Biblica, Inc.™ Used by permission. All rights reserved worldwide.

While all stories in this book are true, some names and identifying information in this book have been changed to protect the privacy of the individuals involved.

Design: Cindy Kiple
Interior design: Beth Hagenberg
Images: © andipantz/iStockphoto

ISBN 978-0-8308-3756-4 (print)
ISBN 978-0-8308-9577-9 (digital)

Printed in the United States of America ∞

Library of Congress Cataloging-in-Publication Data

Gordon, Wayne.
  Making neighborhoods whole : a handbook for Christian community
development / Wayne Gordon and John Perkins.
      pages cm
  Includes bibliographical references.
  ISBN 978-0-8308-3756-4 (pbk. : alk. paper)
  1. Church work with the poor--United States. 2. Christian Community
Development Association. 3. Community development--Religious
aspects—Christianity. I. Perkins, John, 1930- II. Title.

BV639.P6G68 2013
261.8'32--dc23
                                                                    2013024001

P	20	19	18	17	16	15	14	13	12	11	10	9	8	7	6	5	4	3
Y	30	29	28	27	26	25	24	23	22	21	20	19	18	17	16	15		

We dedicate this book to CCDA pioneers

who have gone home to be with the Lord:

Lem Tucker, Tom Skinner,

Spencer Perkins, Peggy Lupton,

Bill Brown and Glen Kehrein

CONTENTS

FOREWORD

When we were first starting our work in Philadelphia, a buddy of mine asked, "Have you ever heard of the CCDA? It's your tribe!"

I hadn't heard of the Christian Community Development Association then, but looking back now, it's hard to imagine the last twenty years without the CCDA. In the early days of The Simple Way, we started piling into cars and going to conferences, reading every CCDA book we could get our hands on, and visiting CCDA ministries whenever we got the chance. I even took my mom with me so she could hear older folks talking the same way we do and have some of her fears expunged. (It worked.) The CCDA has become one of those places where we are reminded that we are not crazy—or at least not alone. It has become our tribe.

I eventually was honored to serve on the board of directors for the CCDA and I can remember us wrestling with what we were becoming. Was the CCDA a movement? An organization? An association? I remember us asking whether it could evolve and stay relevant. Would the ideas get stale? Would it see itself age, like much of the church, and lose the next generation?

On the one hand, the roots of the CCDA are in the Civil Rights Movement, its mission of reconciliation originating from helping black folks and white folks see each other as more than equals, as family. But over the years I have been thrilled, sometimes stunned, to see the CCDA continue to innovate and expand its vision—without ever losing its original fire or its original foundation.

I've seen the CCDA navigate the fragile path between preserving its historic roots and allowing itself to permeate a new generation, whose vision for reconciliation goes far beyond blacks and whites and whose issues are ever new: gun violence, restorative justice, prison reform, immigration . . .

But the CCDA is the place where we wrestle with these issues, and we get a wisdom beyond our own. As you will see in this book, the power of the CCDA is young and old together, as the prophets said:

> Your sons and daughters will prophesy,
>   your old men will dream dreams,
> your young men will see visions. (Joel 2:28)

This book is filled with the dreams and visions of men and women, young and old, all colors of skin, dreaming the dreams of God for our neighborhoods and for our world.

The CCDA is one of the most promising movements in North America, and increasingly around the globe. Thousands upon thousands of folks have been inspired by this eclectic cross-cultural, intergenerational, transdenominational movement. It has now become the largest association of faith-based organizations and faith-fueled activists in North America. And one of my favorite things about the CCDA is that it has "teeth." It has DNA. It has these distinctive values we call the "Eight Key Components" defining who we are and what we are about.

So much of our culture—call it "postmodernity" or whatever—
is resistant to formulas, brands and protocols. I remember
hearing someone say that trying to nail down mission statements or doctrinal statements today is like trying to nail Jell-o
to the wall. But while we don't need universal blueprints that
we try to impose everywhere, we do need some tools we share
in common as we build, and we need some training on how
they work. No one is interested in a brand or franchise, but we
are interested in a movement. And that requires some structure
and foundations. One of my heroes, Dorothy Day, often said we
have to be very intentional and very disciplined as we form
communities, because we are trying to create an environment
where it is "easier to be good." And there are many compelling
forces in our world that make it hard to be good, and many
things in our neighborhoods that don't always make it easy to
be good.

Jesus tells a story about the farmer that sows seeds. Some of
them are eaten by birds, some trampled underfoot, some choked
by thorns. But then there is the seed that lands on shallow soil
and shoots up beautifully, then dies quickly because it has no
roots. Over the years we've seen lots of exciting new communities, ministries and organizations get started that are like that
last seed. Their life is beautiful but short-lived, simply because
they never grew roots. The CCDA is the best landing pad I know
of for new communities. Like the seeds that land on fertile soil,
the CCDA helps new expressions grow roots—you can see that
from the fruit. All over the country and around the world, you
can see folks who have grown roots in the CCDA, made the
principles in this book their own and seen some pretty sweet
harvests come from it all.

So while this book is not about formulas, brands or protocols,
it is about identifying and articulating some of the distinctive

ingredients that make for a healthy ministry and a sustainable missional life. Where do we send our kids to school? How do we afford health care? How do we avoid gentrification in our neighborhoods? Should we take government money? Rather than keep toiling away on our own, sometimes we need to stop, admit we don't know exactly what we should do next, and look for some help. The CCDA offers an entire community of friends who have been tilling similar ground for a long, long time.

Like a trellis for the garden, our work needs some structure or the tomato plants will flop over and rot. But too much structure suffocates life rather than supporting growth. Structure is what *Making Neighborhoods Whole* is all about. While the book will help you build on the work of others, it won't suffocate your ministry; it still leaves room for you to be yourself. All through this book are tools that create a healthy trellis for ministry that can weather storms and grow up to produce great fruit.

This book is like the "Greatest Hits" album of the CCDA. Coach and JP have been teaching these ideas since the inception of the movement. But the ideas never get old because innovative new voices keep adapting, articulating and embodying them in fresh ways. The tried-and-true wisdom of the urban ministry veterans of the CCDA are coupled in this book with dozens of other leaders. Their voices harmonize throughout—the "Eight Key Components" for a new generation of Christians committed to Jesus and to changing the world.

"Changing the world" is good, and yet this book is written by folks whose feet have never left their neighborhood. The worlds they're changing are very real places. Coach, JP and all their friends who have contributed to this book are practitioners of what they preach. They are not trying to sell you Kool-aid they aren't drinking. They have taught me and shown me that every neighborhood, no matter how traumatized and forsaken, still has hope. This is the promise we have in Jesus: nothing is beyond redemption.

Sometimes hope gets locked up. Sometimes hope gets held hostage. But on the pages of this book you'll find some of the keys that can set hope free.

So, be inspired by the folks in this book. May they move you, as they have me, to participate in setting hope free again where you are.

Shane Claiborne

1

A TALE OF TWO ACTIVISTS

**Roots of Christian
Community Development**

The telling of any history—whether of an organization, a country, a movement or something else—cannot be considered complete without a prehistory, an account of the significant people and major events and trends that contributed to the official beginning. A thorough history of the United States of America, for example, does not begin on July 4, 1776, but rather with a description of the social and political milieu and of the events (and the people associated with those events) that came to a focal point on that day.

The Christian Community Development Association (CCDA) is no exception. It became an official legal entity in 1989. But to understand the CCDA's history—including the people, events and theological convictions that have contributed to its founding and its evolution—one must go back much further than 1989, perhaps as far back as 1930, when John Perkins was born on a cotton plantation in New Hebron, Mississippi. The context of poverty and injustice in which John was reared became the cauldron in which was formed the concept of Christian community development and the core principles that define the Christian community development movement today.

At the center of the CCDA story lies a deep and abiding intergenerational friendship—a bond, a brotherhood in fact—between the two of us. In the 1960s, at roughly the same time John was being beaten in a jail in Brandon, Mississippi, because of the stand he took for justice and equal rights, Wayne, a high school kid from rural Iowa, awoke in the middle of the night sensing an unmistakable call from God to live and minister among African American people. Both of us believe that, long before we met or even knew of each other, God's hand was at work in our lives, preparing us individually for a time when we would do something together—something significant and lasting—for the sake of countless individuals and for the kingdom of God.

John's Story

I was born on June 16, 1930, in rural Mississippi. When I was just seven months old, my mother died. The cause was determined to be "nutrition deficiency." In essence, my mother starved to death. My father gave me and my four siblings to his mother (my grandmother). She had nineteen other children to look after, so I didn't get much attention, let alone much love.

My immediate and extended family were not exactly churchgoing people. They were, in fact, largely bootleggers and gamblers. The only reason I could not be considered a high school dropout is because I never made it to high school; I dropped out of school in the third grade, never to return. As a teenager, however, I began to think deeply about what it meant to be fully human.

My foray into philosophy was prompted at points by how I was treated. Working all day hauling hay for a white gentleman, for example, I expected to receive a dollar and a half for my labor. Instead I was given fifteen cents. Formal education or not, I knew this was unfair. I began to view poverty as previous generations had viewed slavery—primarily through the lens of economics.

Though the word *redistribution* had yet to enter my vocabulary, the first seeds of Christian community development had been planted: I wanted to help the haulers of hay become owners of the fields.

In the 1940s, my older brother Clyde came back from World War II. Ironically, he survived a deadly war, but within six months of returning to Mississippi he would be dead, killed by a white police officer in a racial incident. I reacted with feelings of hatred and anger, but the incident also planted the seeds for another of the original three components of Christian community development: reconciliation.

Some of my family and friends were afraid that I would end up like my brother, so they urged me to leave Mississippi. I had a cousin who'd migrated to Southern California, so at least I would have something of a base out of which to operate. I left Mississippi at age seventeen and remained in California for ten years.

Though racist attitudes and behavior were far from absent on the West Coast, life there was nothing like what I had experienced back in Mississippi. California was truly a land of new opportunity. I worked for a steel foundry that made cast iron for building houses, and eventually I became one of the company's leaders. In 1951 I married Vera Mae Buckley, and we started a family.

A great job, a nice house, a safe community, a growing family—in many ways I was a black man in pre–Civil Rights America living the American dream. But in time I would realize that I didn't have what I was seeking most: love.

Not just any love, of course. I've never doubted Vera Mae's

love for me. Yet something was missing. I had never known my mother, and I had been virtually anonymous in my grand-mother's overextended household. I met my father when I was four years old. He showed me some personal attention, made me feel as though I mattered, but then he left the next day. I continued to see him from time to time until he died.

I lived with this longing, becoming a workaholic to fill the void through financial success, until the age of twenty-seven. That's when I heard the central message of the gospel:

> I have been crucified with Christ and I no longer live, but Christ lives in me. The life I now live in the body, I live by faith in the Son of God, who loved me and gave himself for me. (Galatians 2:20)

Especially for someone who had grown up without feeling love, without receiving more than a trace of personal attention, that message was stark. Paul's words jumped out at me: I finally recognized that my longing was for a kind of love deeper than any human being could provide. And if there was a God who loved me so much that he sent his Son to die, I wanted to know that God—to worship and follow that God.

Soon I was being discipled and mentored by a much older white man, a Presbyterian Bible teacher, Mr. Lietch, who had a vision to train teachers to carry the gospel message to children in the ghetto. Mr. Lietch stimulated and affirmed my dream to love my people back in Mississippi. He recognized that he could live his ministry dream for the black community in part through me.

He told me, my third-grade education notwithstanding, I had the fastest mind of anybody he'd ever met.

Because it was the words of Scripture that led to my salvation, I developed an immediate and virtually unquenchable thirst for

Bible knowledge. I applied my mind to studying the Bible early every morning. With each day came more revelations. A whole new understanding and vision for life unfolded before me.

I was captivated by the Genesis account of God's changing Abram's name to "Abraham" and making him a father to many generations. Reflecting on my family name back in Mississippi— a name tarnished with the reputation of bootlegging, gambling and crime—I made a commitment to preach and teach the Bible with the hope that God would redeem my family name. Little did I know at the time that a few decades hence people all over the United States, even around the world, would be requesting a speaker by the name of John Perkins. I was reconciled to God and began to do reconciliation with people along racial lines.

Before long I began to build relationships with Christian businessmen and others who were involved in a wide range of Christian activities—from Bible studies to prison ministry to missionary service. I met missionaries returning from the field who loved the black people among whom they served more than they loved white folk. And then one day I accepted an invitation to join a group on a visit to a local prison.

I didn't realize going in that the visit would change my life. I'd thought the inmates would be older men; instead they were young—some of them barely more than children. When I looked at them, I saw myself: these young men looked like me and talked like me, broken grammar and all.

I shared my testimony with about sixty young men—boys really—in a Quonset hut. As I finished, I noticed a couple of the boys in the back shaking and crying uncontrollably. They told me through tears that their lives were like mine, and I knew it was true. These boys struggled with many of the same things I had struggled with, beginning with a lack of love in their lives. They, too, wanted to know Jesus.

I realized that God could take my hunger for Scripture and my desire to share the gospel and turn it into an avocation. I also realized how privileged I was to have a beautiful wife, children, a big house and a great job with a stable company. And I knew—in that very moment in that prison—that I couldn't stay in California.

I felt an instant yearning, a confidence that I had to return to Mississippi, to my roots, humble and unstable as they were. Like Martin Luther, I could do no other. I was destined to relocate—the third and final of the original three Rs of Christian community development.

Vera Mae wasn't so sure. She didn't at first quite understand my desire to return to the very oppression I'd successfully escaped. But she could see that God was working on my heart, and that trumped any skepticism she may have harbored. Truth is, I would never have returned had Vera Mae not supported me in doing so.

I had heard a missionary speak about the parting of the Red Sea, about how the ancient Israelites first had to wade in the water before God parted the water in front of them. So in the fall of 1959 I waded into the waters. I spent six weeks in my childhood home town of New Hebron, and then I returned for good with my family in 1960. We ended up settling in Mendenhall, twenty or so miles to the northeast, where both of us had virtually limitless opportunities to reach people of all ages for Christ.

Vera Mae and I used flannel boards to tell Bible stories to children. I led Bible studies, shared my testimony in churches and taught Sunday school. I told public school principals that if I came to their schools I would talk not just about morality but about my faith in Christ. They invited me anyway.

Among the things I was saved from when I came to Christ was a concern for self-preservation. I didn't care anymore about being wealthy, even though I knew very well the value of money. Many of those I'd befriended in California, including some very wealthy businessmen, considered me a missionary to the lost, and they provided financial support for me to minister in Mendenhall. One wealthy woman who considered me a son gathered people together to hear me speak when I returned to the West Coast from time to time. I started a newsletter to keep my supporters informed; my mailing list grew from seven hundred to nearly ten thousand.

I was leading Bible studies at least two or three nights a week and speaking in schools almost every day. As more and more young people in and around Mendenhall came to Christ, our ministry spawned a church. But we knew that if we were going to have a major impact in the area, we couldn't do it alone.

Most of the young people in Mendenhall who'd become Christians were leaving for greener pastures at their first opportunity. In fact, this poor community was getting even poorer. I told Vera Mae that we would have to stay long enough to build a new generation of leadership. This would entail challenging young people to develop a love for God and a love for people that was deeper than their love of consumerism. It would mean developing indigenous leaders—challenging people to return to Mendenhall after going to college, bringing their leadership skills and abilities back to the community. Among the many who took this challenge to heart were Artis Fletcher, the pastor of Mendenhall Bible Church since 1974, and Dolphus Weary, who led many of Mendenhall's outreach ministries for several years.

Something else was happening in Mississippi and elsewhere in the 1960s South that would redirect the focus of our ministry. The Civil Rights movement was gaining strength. A turning point for us was the killing of Medgar Evers in Jackson, Mississippi, in June 1963. It was no longer natural for me to be mis-

treated, nor could I stand idly by while others were discrimi-
nated against based on race.

I was committed to nonviolent action, so I began taking part
in efforts to register voters, which seemed a natural thing to do
after having had a taste of true freedom and equality. Vera Mae
and I opened our home to civil rights workers, which led occasionally to us fearing for our lives, or at least for our safety.

This brand of social action did not sit well with my supporters back in California, most of whom wanted me to stick
with a strictly spiritual message. By 1967, most of my original
supporters had cut me off. But I found others to take their place.

I didn't stop at registering voters. Children were dying of diabetes and other illnesses. In the midst of talk about government
grants and health care surveys and feasibility studies, Vera Mae
proclaimed, "The need is now. We can't wait." And we didn't.

Our emphasis on wholistic ministry (which would be foundational for the CCDA years later) was beginning to take root.
Our health center in Mendenhall grew out of the Voice of
Calvary church ministry. It welcomed any and all doctors and
nurses who could help, even if they only stayed for six months
to satisfy the requirements of a medical school scholarship. The
medical care available at our health center was nothing like
what white folk had, but it was more than what had existed
before for black people, which was nothing.

My social activism came to a head in 1970. Earlier during a
boycott in Mendenhall, a boy had been arrested and beaten in
jail; I didn't want it to happen to anyone else. When I found out
the police were coming to a store in downtown Mendenhall for
another boy who'd had too much to drink, I got there first and
took him home. Before I knew it, I saw flashing lights in my rear
view mirror, but I didn't stop till I had crossed the tracks into
the boy's black community.

The police took the boy in for disturbing the peace. I went to our church, where the choir was getting ready for our Christmas program. Nearly twenty of us went to the Mendenhall jail, hoping to make bond so the boy wouldn't get beaten. I was arrested and put in jail, where I was beaten. The beating included a fork in my nose and punches to my mid-section, producing internal injuries that cause me trouble still today.

Two months later, after a successful protest and boycott of stores in Mendenhall, I was arrested on Highway 49 in Rankin County. I was taken to the jail in Brandon, where I was once again beaten. On the floor of the Brandon Jail, I realized the extent of the damage that racism had inflicted on white people. I vowed never to hate white people. Instead, I made a commitment to work for reconciliation, to love white people even if they hated me.

Nevertheless, from that point on, I feared for my life. It's partly why in 1973 we moved to Jackson, where I live and minister today. We picked up in Jackson where we'd left off in Mendenhall, launching a new ministry in 1975 with a similar if not identical vision.

Wayne's Story

Long before we'd ever even heard of each other, John and I chose the same life verse:

> I have been crucified with Christ and I no longer live, but Christ lives in me. The life I now live in the body, I live by faith in the Son of God, who loved me and gave himself for me. (Galatians 2:20)

In January 1970, I was a high school junior. One night, barely a month before John was beaten in Brandon Jail, I awoke my mother at 1 a.m. to tell her that I'd had a strong sense that God was calling me to minister in the African American community.

I felt it so strongly I wanted to quit high school and get started.

My mother advocated for patience, but she took me seriously, encouraging me to meet with our pastor. During that meeting, our pastor walked to his bookshelf and pulled out the book *Black and Free* by Tom Skinner. To this day, I consider it something of a minor miracle that this rural Iowa pastor had even heard of Skinner's book. I devoured that book as if it were written just for me. It answered all my questions and addressed all my concerns about how white people can be effective ministering in a "Negro" community. Among other things, it permanently etched the concept of "paternalism" in my mind as something to avoid.

My sense of calling never diminished from that day. If anything, it grew stronger. I spent the summer of 1970 ministering in an inner-city African American community in Chicago. In December I attended InterVarsity's Urbana Student Missions Conference, at which Tom Skinner was the keynote speaker. I considered him my "empowerer"; I attended all of Tom's workshops and soaked up his every word, though I never once approached him.

In the fall of 1971 I enrolled at Wheaton College, largely because it was close to Chicago. Whenever Tom Skinner got anywhere near the Windy City, I showed up to hear him. I never asked questions, though, because I didn't know what to ask. I just sat at Tom's feet and learned.

While at Wheaton I took advantage of opportunities to volunteer in Chicago. Meanwhile, in 1973, at the historic Chicago Declaration Conference, evangelicals declared their support for social action and thus for wholistic Christian ministry.

During my final semester at Wheaton, in 1975, I went to chapel to hear John Perkins, a speaker whose name I'd never heard. I was moved almost to tears as John described his ministry. It was everything I had been thinking about, dreaming about, preparing for.

Shortly after graduating I relocated to North Lawndale, one of Chicago's poorest and most crime-infested areas. I became a teacher and coach at Farragut High School with no thought of ever being a pastor. I merely wanted to lead Bible studies among high school youth, lead them to Christ and love them wholistically, as Christ loves them. (Eventually the youth I was working with convinced Anne and me to start a church, and they persuaded me to be its pastor. The full story of the early years of Lawndale Community Church is told in my book *Real Hope in Chicago*.) It was at Farragut where I earned the moniker "Coach," a nickname I've never relinquished.

More than a few people—white and black alike—called me crazy for moving to such a dangerous part of town. But I was convinced it was what I was called to do. I was candid about this calling with Anne, the woman I wanted to date; I told her that if she could not see herself living in Lawndale, there would be no sense in dating—that was a deal breaker. Anne was not deterred, though.

I had met Anne at a funeral in Indianapolis; she was the girl of my dreams. I fell in love with her immediately; she was everything I had hoped for: strong character, deep faith and a discerning spirit that has helped me tremendously over the years. God has done exceedingly abundantly beyond what we have asked or thought—that is what Anne has been for me. We were married in June of 1977.

Even though both of us had second thoughts when our house in Lawndale was broken into on our first night there together, we stayed the course. That night I thought God was possibly giving me a sign that bringing my wonderful wife to live with me in Lawndale was a mistake. When I expressed this to her she

responded, "I love you, and I want to live here." Thank God for
Anne, or we probably wouldn't be living here today.

About a year after my first encounter with John Perkins, I had
my second, when I read his book *Let Justice Roll Down*. Although
some in the Christian press had reported on John's beating in
Brandon Jail in 1970, for the most part he'd ministered in obscurity for ten years; it's a point I like to make today among
those, including mentees, who are in pursuit of instant recognition. His first book, however, put John on the map. This book
really crystallized how to help the people of Lawndale; it was
comprehensive, wholistic and nonpaternalistic. I knew in my
heart that this was the philosophy of ministry God was calling
me to.

Neither of us knew in 1976 how tightly our lives and ministries
would in time be woven together. The Christian Community
Development Association was still more than a decade away
from being formally founded. But its true story cannot be told
without recounting this tale of two activists.

2

CHRISTIAN COMMUNITY DEVELOPMENT COMES TOGETHER

The CCDA's Early Years

In the late 1970s various churches and other organizations were doing community development work in urban areas and elsewhere. Most didn't call it that though. By and large, they didn't know what others were doing; consequently there was very little sharing of wisdom and experience.

Nevertheless, the ministries John had begun in Mendenhall and in Jackson, Mississippi—ministries that for several years had operated in obscurity—were fast becoming models for a wholistic approach. Leaders were beginning to find one another and, in some cases, to work together.

Based largely on the recognition gained from their bestselling books,[1] John and Ron Sider began collaborating to proclaim an evangelical gospel message that took seriously issues of justice and responsibility for the world's poor. They formed a friendship as they spoke in various venues around the country, and more and more people listened; the movement welcomed some highly regarded allies, including British scholar and author John R. W. Stott.

Let Justice Roll Down represented exactly the kind of ministry I (Coach) was certain God had called me to do. Then, in 1978, we started the church in Lawndale, with me as its pastor.

One of the first things we did as a new church was survey the neighborhood to find out why people didn't attend church. The response boiled down to four factors.

- One, they felt they didn't have nice enough clothes to wear.

- Two, they felt embarrassed because they had no money to put in the offering plate.

- Three, they were angry at God because of the disappointments they had faced in life.

- Four, they thought the church was irrelevant because there were lots of churches yet nothing ever seemed to change.

We did our best to address all four concerns.

- We didn't have (and thirty-five years later still don't have) a dress code, even an informal or unspoken one. People are free to come as they are. In fact, if anyone feels out of place at our church, it's those who come all decked out.

- We have never passed offering plates. There's a box at the side for those who want to give.

- We've considered anger at God a communication problem, which we've addressed through the serious study of Scripture.

- And from the beginning we were committed to making a tangible difference in the quality of life in our community—from housing and health care to legal aid and education and much, much more. As the young people pointed out, if Jesus calls us to love our neighbors, it's our job as a church to love and serve our neighborhood.

Jubilee

As the ministries in Mendenhall and Jackson matured and as I (John) got more and more opportunities to speak in the United States and overseas, I met many people with whom my message and the approach it represented struck a responsive chord. I naturally tried on an informal basis to connect people with others who were trying to do similar ministry work, but my board of advisors felt we should try to make a more formal effort to network people. They began advocating for a national movement.

This led to two events to help teach and equip people working among the poor—called Jubilee conferences—in Jackson, the first in 1980 and the second in 1982. Their purpose was to bring like-minded people together for encouragement, inspiration and the sharing of knowledge. (In this respect these Jubilee events were precursors to the Christian Community Development Association.) Some five hundred people attended the first event. Among the keynote speakers was Prison Fellowship founder Chuck Colson. About seven hundred people attended in 1982. Speakers that year included Tony Campolo (founder of the Evangelical Association for the Promotion of Education), Tony Evans (founding pastor of Oak Cliff Bible Fellowship in Dallas, Texas), Tom Skinner and Bruce Thielemann. Coach and Anne were among those attending this second event.

Up to that point I (Coach) had not met John in person, but at the 1982 Jubilee Conference, Anne and I had lunch with him. We felt the Spirit of God moving at this event, not just in our lives but for everyone there. People were reading books and sharing information. We spoke with Lem Tucker, the executive director of Voice of Calvary in Jackson, the ministry John had started. Together we asked, "Is this a movement?"

I got as much advice as I could from others at this event because, frankly, ministry in Lawndale was very, very hard. Anne and I already had one child and we were expecting another. Our house had been broken into at least ten times. I was doing substitute teaching, and to say we were living on a shoestring budget would be to make it seem easier than it was. Suffice it to say that every penny counted. We had about forty people attending the church, most of them youth who were much poorer than we were. It was natural to have doubts as to whether we should keep going, especially when so many people around us were telling us to give up. We needed the encouragement that the 1982 Jubilee event provided.

Return to California, Renewal in Chicago

Prior to the 1982 Jubilee event, I (John) had moved my family from Mississippi back to California. Three young indigenous leaders I had mentored—Lem Tucker in Jackson, and Artis Fletcher and Dolphus Weary in Mendenhall—were ready to take flight on their own. We settled in Pasadena, where we established the Harambee Christian Family Center and the John Perkins Foundation for Reconciliation and Development.

These ministries were further expressions of various aspects of the Christian community development philosophy. Our ministry included youth outreach and Bible clubs. We also had a gym. We started a school that was incorporated as a nonprofit. Vera Mae resumed doing what she's done everywhere we've been—starting Good News clubs and using flannel graphs to lead many children to Christ.

Meanwhile, the 1982 Jubilee event convinced me (Coach) that I needed, as much as possible, to surround myself with people who could help guide Lawndale Community Church and its ministries. Shortly after Jubilee we set up an advisory board that included John, Tom Skinner, Dolphus Weary, Chicago pastor Bill Leslie, Urban Ministries founder Mel Banks and seminary professor and thought leader Ray Bakke. Pat McCaskey from the Chicago Bears and linebacker Mike Singletary were also a part of the group, as were several people from Lawndale and some pastors from the suburbs. This board convened twice a year, starting in 1983, to help our church leaders and me process how we were to live out this calling on our lives.

The church was saving every nickel and dime we could, and in 1983 we were finally able to purchase a building that we planned to convert to a gym. Around Thanksgiving of that year, an article about our small but growing ministry appeared in the *Chicago Tribune*. It included a photo of balloons being released at the dedication of our new building. People at Christ Church of Oakbrook saw the article, and soon Christ Church became LCC's first big supporter. It still supports us today.

After two years of getting priceless guidance from LCC's advisory board, we began to think that we were being selfish by keeping this to ourselves. We wanted others to hear what we were hearing, to learn what we were learning about ministry, to have access to the same guidance we were receiving. So we turned these advisory board meetings into mini-conferences, held annually at Lawndale, beginning in the spring of 1985 and continuing through 1988.

We took care of all formal business in the morning and then opened the afternoon to all who wanted to come and learn. The hours between 1 p.m. and 6 p.m. were filled with keynote speakers, panel discussions, and workshops on specific topics. We spoke in terms of "urban ministry." (At that time, "Christian community development" was not in our vernacular.) Average attendance ranged from 300 to 400.

Looking back, I recognize that the structure of these events laid the groundwork for future CCDA conferences, though at the time the idea of the CCDA had yet to be born.

In addition to these meetings in Lawndale, we like-minded people looked for other opportunities to get together. Whenever there was a conference or event sponsored by World Vision, Campus Crusade or some other Christian organization, those of us who were active in inner-city ministry would sit around and compare notes, sometimes for hours at a time. I recall conversations with Mary Nelson from Bethel New Life in Chicago, Ron Spann from Church of the Messiah in Detroit, Eddie Edwards from Joy of Jesus in Detroit, Glen Kehrein from Circle Urban Ministries in Chicago, and Bob Lupton from FCS Urban Ministries in Atlanta.

It seemed Lem Tucker was always there with us, and during this time I got especially close to him. In 1987, I joined the board of Voice of Calvary, which only broadened my vision for what cross-pollination among similar ministries could accomplish. Lem and I talked about getting all these urban ministry folks together for our own event, something bigger and more ambitious than what we'd been doing at Lawndale.

If I could point to a moment when the idea of the CCDA was born, I would point to the time Lem visited me in Chicago. We had lunch, and as we sat together in my kitchen we found ourselves dreaming about starting something that might be called the Christian Community Development Association. Lem continued to have these meetings with a few other people throughout the country. The first step would be to convene a special meeting to see if those who had been getting together informally wanted to go ahead with it.

The Founding Conference

Lem's first step was to speak with John to get his input on our proposal. At the time John was my hero and advisor, but he was not yet my mentor and best friend, both of which he would eventually become. I was closer then to Tom Skinner, who made sure to let me know every time he came to Chicago and often preached at Lawndale Community Church.

John gave his full support to the idea, and in February 1989 we convened a group of about fifty urban ministry leaders at Chicago's O'Hare airport. We had by this time begun using the term "Christian community development," describing it primarily in terms of John's three Rs: relocation, reconciliation and redistribution. Lem led that first meeting, at which the group expressed its favor for formally launching an association. Nothing was set in stone, but the plan called for Lem to serve as president. John took me aside and said he wanted me to be vice president.

Over the next few months a smaller group of fifteen to twenty people convened at Lawndale to plan the details of a national gathering, scheduled for October. Sadly, Lem would not be a part of this gathering. In March of 1989, he was diagnosed with a fast-spreading form of cancer (American Burkitt's Lymphoma). Three months later, on June 16, he died.

We pressed on. Although the CCDA was not yet officially incorporated, our first national conference took place October 26-29 at Lawndale Community Church. About 140 people attended. On the first night John shared the vision of Christian community development and how forming an association would enable people to support one another. On the second night Bob Lupton gave a talk on family, marriage and ministry, in which he spoke very candidly about struggles he and his wife, Peggy, had experienced living and working in the inner city. Not only was this talk groundbreaking in its own right, but it laid the foundation for CCDA to address issues honestly and also to deal openly with the struggles of family life, especially as they relate to the struggles of ministry. (This candor comes through in several of this book's essays.)

At our first conference, the CCDA made a commitment to consider spouses and children in all discussions and ministry directions. We wanted our association to be a place for total honesty, because we knew that's what it would take to get the support we all needed from one another.

By and large, the conference was structured very much like the Jubilee events had been. People could attend workshops to address the topics in which they were most interested, whether education, health care, youth ministry or something else. On the third and final night I gave the plenary address after being "elected" CCDA president earlier in the day. I had no idea I'd even been nominated; I'd left an afternoon board meeting for a few minutes, and I returned to discover I was president. Bob Lupton assured me this would be largely a figurehead role. In his words, "All we want is a do-nothing president." I wasn't so sure.

I suspect I was chosen for this role for two main reasons. First, the ministry in Lawndale had experienced visible success. The church at that time had grown to about 150 people, and we'd moved into a larger building. We had a full-scale gym, a medical clinic with five or so doctors, and several other ministries at various stages of development. But second, I could testify that ministry had been hard—joyful, but hard. And in 1989 I could say that it still was hard. And in 2013 I continue to say it.

Aptly enough, the theme for my first plenary address was, "It ain't easy, but it can happen."

The Founding Leadership

I (John) was selected as chairman of the CCDA board. Perhaps the best thing about Coach and me being chosen for these leadership roles was that it would provide the opportunity our friendship—a brotherhood, actually—to continue to bloom and grow.

Eight people came to our first conference already having committed to serve as founding board members. We selected four more from those in attendance, bringing the total number of charter board members to twelve: the two of us and Spencer Perkins (from Jackson, Mississippi), Glen Kehrein (from Chicago), Mary Nelson (from Chicago), Bob Lupton (from Atlanta), Ron Spann (from Detroit), Herman Moten (from Tampa), Kathy Dudley (from Dallas), Elizar Pagan (from St. Charles, Illinois), Bob Penton (from Tacoma, Washington), and Jana Webb (from Monrovia, California). The Perkins Foundation (including board members Bill Gregg II, Gary Vanderark, Al Whittaker, Norm Nason, Roy Rogers and Howard Ahmanson) provided both leadership and financial support aimed toward officially incorporating the CCDA as a 501c3. Cynder Rocker Baptist, a board member at the Perkins Foundation, did most of the legwork. World Vision, Howard and Roberta Ahmanson, and the Pew Foundation also provided some seed money.

Because all this was happening in California, that's where we gained official recognition late in 1989. Since Coach was president, however, the CCDA's offices moved to Chicago. We operated under California bylaws until 2006, when we officially became an Illinois nonprofit.

The First Ten Years

Over the next ten years, the CCDA would grow and change in many ways. The first two conferences were held at Chicago churches. Most attendees lodged with friends or church members. At our third conference (1991 in Atlanta), we met for the first time in a hotel (the cheapest one we could find), and about four hundred attended. Each year throughout our first decade, the numbers increased. We reached a thousand attendees at the fifth annual conference (1993 in Jackson), 1,500 in 1995 (Denver), and 2,000 in 1997 (Birmingham, Alabama).

Five staff people—Donna Holt, Adonya Little, Cheryl Cornelius, Joanie Perkins-Potter and Charris Dower—were pivotal in the early growth of the organization.

In 1994, we published a membership directory that listed 201 organizations, representing twenty-two states and three foreign countries. Ethiopian Jember Tefera became the first overseas person to give a conference address. Whereas in the beginning, the budget for the annual conference was negligible, the budget for our tenth annual conference in 1998 was $186,000.

Each year keynote speakers delivered insightful and inspirational addresses, some of which became landmark moments in the history of the CCDA. At the second conference in 1992, for example, Tom Skinner spoke on how ministry can become a monster, in that we spend so much time and energy on structure that there is little left over for ministry. This helped the CCDA leadership and membership stay focused on the grassroots. Another landmark message was Noel Castellanos' "More Color, More Better" (1992), in which he challenged a mostly black and white CCDA to reach out to Latinos and other ethnic groups.

In addition to its annual conference, the CCDA began to coordinate other events, each focusing on a single, highly relevant topic. These included a housing seminar in 1991, a workshop on fundraising and board development in 1994, a youth conference (attended by four hundred youth) in 1997, and a symposium on welfare reform, also in 1997. After the publication of Coach's book *Real Hope for Chicago,* we launched our American cities campaign: over the next five years the two of us together visited dozens of cities (seventy in the United States alone) where CCDA ministries were active. We went as observers and encouragers, offering advice wherever and whenever we could, and spreading the CCDA approach to ministry.

Along the way we experienced significant loss. Tom Skinner died of leukemia in 1994, exactly five years and one day after we lost Lem Tucker. Spencer Perkins, John's son, died suddenly of heart failure in January 1998. At the time of his passing, Spencer was director of the International Study Center at Voice of Calvary in Jackson. A champion of racial reconciliation, he'd coauthored (with Chris Rice) the 1993 book *More Than Equals: Racial Healing for the Sake of the Gospel.*[2]

We celebrated our tenth anniversary as a ministry association at our eleventh annual conference in 1999. For the first time, we started on a Wednesday night, making it a four-day event instead of three. We met at Moody Bible Institute and Moody Memorial Church in Chicago. The lineup of speakers included such luminaries and celebrities as Tony Campolo, Ray Bakke, Tony Evans, Ron Sider, Leah Gaskin Fitchue and Jawanza Kunjufu. Up to then, the most we'd drawn to an annual conference was 2,200 the previous year in St. Louis. Our tenth-anniversary celebration drew 3,500. In addition to the usual substance, it truly was a celebratory event. The CCDA was riding high. Little did we know that troubling waters lay just around the river bend.

3

THE STATE OF CHRISTIAN COMMUNITY DEVELOPMENT

Recent Past to Next Horizon

While the tenth anniversary conference in 1999 was an overwhelming success for the CCDA, the 2000 conference at New York Presbyterian Church in Queens, New York City, proved financially crippling. We had high expectations. Some 3,500 had come to Chicago the year before, and now it was a new millennium, and we were meeting in our country's biggest city. We learned too late how prohibitive the costs of lodging in the Big Apple were for many of our regular attendees. And the CCDA's overall presence in New York was not very strong—certainly nothing like it was in Chicago, where it all began. Only 1,300 attended the New York conference, and the CCDA took a financial hit of $40,000. Given that we were operating on a shoestring budget, we had no choice but to cut hours and pay for our staff members.

Our troubles were not over. In September 2001 we both went to Dallas to meet with the people organizing the conference there in October. Among them was CCDA founding board member Kathy Dudley. Kathy was the founder of Voice of Hope, a Christian community center in Dallas that operates on principles of self-help, spiritual enrichment and urban renewal. The purpose of our trip was to plan details for the conference, but we also had an issue to address: the venue for the event, the Adams Mark Hotel, was being boycotted by the NAACP due to race-related concerns.

We were meeting at a coffee shop in Dallas the morning two planes hit the World Trade Center buildings in New York. Everything changed. We wondered whether we should even go ahead with the 2001 conference. Among the many factors under consideration was that the CCDA could not afford to take another financial loss.

We decided to proceed. Understandably, conference presentations were shaped overwhelmingly by the events of that awful September morning. Yet a great spirit prevailed. We were pleasantly surprised at the attendance of 1,600, which enabled us to finish the year in the black—barely, and only thanks to financial contributions from board members, some of whom were concerned the CCDA would not survive.

The plain and simple truth is that the CCDA was struggling to stay in business. So much of our financial viability was based on conference attendance, which for two years in a row was down dramatically. These yearly conferences were always filled with such great content and energy that not many knew what was going on behind the scenes.

And, frankly, I (Wayne) I was burning out. In 1998, after weeks of agonizing and getting counsel from people like John Perkins and Ray Bakke, our family decided to take a three-year leave of absence from Lawndale and move to Naperville, Illinois. Without question this was the toughest decision of my entire life. I loved living in Lawndale and experiencing life together with our community as we had for the past twenty-three years.

We moved for a variety of reasons. I was, for one thing, feeling a need to be more present for my wife and children, and moving from Lawndale seemed like a way to give more focused attention to my family. I had also been invited to teach in the Doctor of Ministry program at Eastern Baptist Theological Seminary in Philadelphia, during which time I'd also be studying for my doctorate. This would take three years and would require more attention than my schedule in Lawndale would permit. Meanwhile, we felt the need for some more networking on behalf of the CCDA, which would involve, among other things, a thirty-six-city tour. Given all these special circumstances, I was growing tired and feeling a need to be refreshed spiritually, something that didn't seem possible in Lawndale at that time.

This move, it seemed to me, was a test of my strong commitment to relocation as a value for community development. Over time I had become guilty of unmercifully judging others who were involved themselves in a community without living there. As I studied and preached from 1 John, I discovered the last verse of the epistle ends with these words: "Dear children, keep yourselves from idols." I realized that I had perhaps made relocation a god and an idol in my life.

At the same time that I took my leave from Lawndale, I submitted my resignation as president of CCDA. But it was not accepted. So I pressed on through the desert, returning to Lawndale in 2001.

Seeds of Growth

Despite the difficult times, some important seeds of growth were planted in 2001. Realizing that we had arrived at a point where we could no longer operate informally and without something that at least resembled a business plan, we hired R. K. Nobles & Associates to do an organizational audit. That process proved extremely helpful in moving our organizational structure toward a true association. Among other things, we decided to hire a CEO, develop a strategic plan, separate the conference budget from the CCDA's annual budget, adopt a policy governing model for the board and bring our database management to state-of-the-art level.

After an extensive national search, in the fall of 2002 we hired Gordon Murphy as CEO. He had been serving as president of Opportunity International, a nonprofit organization that provides small business loans, savings, insurance and training to people working their way out of poverty in the developing world. It would not be an overstatement to say that Gordon rescued the CCDA. He arrived too late in the year to have any real influence on the 2002 conference in Pasadena, which also lost money. But before long his influence and expertise would have a significant impact.

For one thing, Gordon knew how to raise money—to the tune of hundreds of thousands of dollars, much of it in the form of grants from foundations that supported the kinds of ministry that member organizations were doing. He also developed our sponsorship program for the annual conferences to a point where today many organizations will pay thousands of dollars in exchange for visibility at the conference. (This was not just about the CCDA being financially viable. From the vantage point of sponsoring organizations, it was an investment that helped them to reach new people and to achieve their ministry goals.)

Gordon Murphy is a perfect example of how CCDA ministries can make use of the talents of those who care about ministry but are not necessarily committed to all of the CCDA's eight key components. To put it plainly, Gordon was a white guy from the suburbs who had no intention of relocating or running an urban ministry. But he was fully committed to helping the CCDA succeed not just as a ministry but also as a financial entity. In fact he recognized, as we all should, that usually the two go together.

Gordon committed to giving five years to the CCDA, but thankfully he agreed to stay for a few more years as a consultant and advisor to his successor, our current CEO, Noel Castellanos. Noel took over in 2007 and is taking the organization to a new level in terms of both ministry and financial stability.

Noel and his wife, Marianne, reside in the Mexican section of South Lawndale, also known as "Little Village." They have lived the CCDA vision their whole lives. Specifically, they've lived "in the 'hood" for thirty years, and Noel has pastored a church in Little Village. Noel joined the CCDA staff in 2004 with the task of forming and running the CCDA Institute, whose purpose is to provide detailed training in the eight key components of Christian community development. In 2005, with Noel providing leadership, the CCDA Institute visited five cities, including Los Angeles, Philadelphia and Dallas. Not long after he began as CEO, Noel also started what we call "cafés," in which he travels to cities to meet with people who are interested in ministry, sharing with them the basics of the CCDA approach. In the last few years Noel has conducted café meetings in nearly a hundred cities, maybe more.

In 2003, John transitioned into the role of board chair emeritus, and Wayne took over as president and chairman of the board. In 2009, Barbara Williams-Skinner (Tom's wife, who's supported CCDA in many ways, including as a keynote speaker at seven of our annual conferences) became board chair, a role she held until 2013 when Leroy Barber, president of Mission Year, took over. Wayne has continued as president, with the job description consisting mainly of promulgating the CCDA philosophy and developing ministry leaders, leaving Noel to run the day-to-day operation.

Signs of Growth

The CCDA's growth over the past decade or so is reflected in part by its annual budget, which has grown from just over $500,000 in 2003 to more than a million dollars each year since 2010. But the indicators of the CCDA's growth are not limited to financial ones.

Although the CCDA has come to be associated with urban ministry, its key components apply in any demographic setting. In 2002 we held our first rural conference in Chestnut Ridge, West Virginia. Among the speakers were John, Wayne and Dolphus Weary. We've held several events since, usually a day before the annual conference in a rural area near the city in which it is scheduled. These events have, among other accomplishments, helped the CCDA build inroads among Native Americans. Taken together with the Institute and the cafés, our organization has gained visibility and extended its impact as a result.

In 2010 the CCDA partnered with Northern Baptist Theological Seminary in suburban Chicago to start a Master of Divinity program with a focus on community development. The program features several full-tuition John Perkins scholarships. That same year, Northern started a Doctor of Ministry program in Christian community development, codirected by John and Wayne.

Also in 2010, in conjunction with the annual conference in Chicago, the CCDA offered its more than two thousand conference visitors the opportunity to visit ministry sites in Chicago. We called them "rolling workshops," as people could visit several sites throughout the day. Three years later, we still hear people say that this one day changed their lives. Why? Because they came to the conference discouraged, and seeing ministries that after years of struggle had renovated homes, built gyms and started medical clinics gave them both inspiration and hope.

A Bright Future

All the two of us ever wanted for the CCDA was to bring together believers united by common ministry goals and a common ministry theology and philosophy. We wanted people and ministries to have extensive opportunities to share what they have learned with others for the good of the kingdom of God, instead of keeping it to themselves. We envisioned ministries throughout the United States and around the world being stronger and more effective because of the CCDA than they could ever be without it. And we wanted to spread a philosophy of ministry that we feel is both ambitious and firmly rooted in Scripture. We found the results of a 2007 impact survey encouraging. Three-fourths of the respondents said they felt connected to the CCDA. Over 90 percent reported having read and been influenced by CCDA-recommended authors, and 97 percent said they would recommend CCDA to others.

We are confident that the CCDA's future is bright. The CCDA's reputation is strong and still growing. Attendance at our annual conference in recent years has remained strong and steady at about 2,500, although we got to 3,200 at our twenty-second annual event in Chicago in 2010. We have over the years served more than a thousand churches or ministry organizations, and some 15,000 people are active with our association. And because of our emphasis on developing young leaders, we are fully confident that the CCDA will long outlast those who gave it birth and guided it to maturity.

Most of all, we are profoundly grateful to God for how this

venture has brought the two of us together—across the miles and across the years—as brothers in Christ and best friends. It's become a tradition at the annual CCDA conference for John to lead a Bible study every morning from 9 to 10. In recent years, Wayne has joined him. The two of us together. Leading. Teaching. Sharing experiences. Encouraging others. That's all we ever wanted to do and how we hope to be remembered.

The philosophy known as Christian community development was not developed in a classroom. These biblical, practical principles evolved from years of living and working among the poor. John first developed this philosophy in Mississippi; since that time over a thousand communities around the United States and abroad have benefited from the concept.

Christian community development has eight essential components that have evolved over forty years. The first three are based on John's three R's of community development: relocation, reconciliation and redistribution. The rest have been developed by many Christians working together and dialoguing extensively to find ways to rebuild poor neighborhoods. The balance of the book is a description of the eight key components, and how they are being wrestled with today by practitioners around the globe.

4

RELOCATION

The concept of relocation has, unlike some of our eight key components, been associated with Christian community development from the beginning. It is one of John's "3 Rs." The concept of relocation is best understood in terms of what we call a "theology of presence"—a theology that lies at the heart of God's relationship with humanity.

The incarnation—God's coming to earth in human form to live and breathe and walk and work and minister among us—illustrates God's desire to be present with those he has created. We read in Matthew 1:23 that among the names Jesus would be called is "Immanuel," which means "God with us." We read in John 1:14 that "the Word became flesh and made his dwelling among us." We read in Philippians 2:6-7 that Jesus,

> being in very nature God,
> > did not consider equality with God something to be
> > > used to his own advantage;
> rather, he made himself nothing
> > by taking the very nature of a servant,
> > being made in human likeness.

Jesus showed his love by becoming human and pitching his tent among us.

Jesus tells his apostles that the Father will give them "another advocate to help you and be with you forever" (John 14:16). And at the end of Matthew's Gospel he says to the remaining eleven apostles, "Surely I am with you always, to the very end of the age."

It's a clear and recurring theme in Scripture that God desires to be present with his children. The principle of relocation, so foundational to the CCDA from the beginning, lies at the core of Christian theology. Within the Christian community development movement, we encourage relocation in order to practice this central theology of presence.

Relocation Defined

In defining *relocation,* it's important first of all to point out what we do *not* want it to mean or imply. The word has been around since the beginning of the Christian community development movement, but if we were starting over, we would likely try to find a different word.

Relocation as a term carries with it some negative connotations. Some Native Americans, for example, associate the term with being rounded up and placed on reservations against their will. Fortunately, the resulting misunderstandings and hurt feelings have been clarified over time, and Native American participation in the CCDA has been on the rise.

Another problem with the word *relocation* is that it can be interpreted as supporting a paternalistic approach to community development. "Relocation" as we want it to be understood is not about wealthy people from the suburbs going into poverty-stricken areas to save the day with their supposed expertise. It's certainly not about white folks treating ethnic minorities like projects or problems to be solved. In fact, as we will discuss in more detail later in the book, we believe that the people in the best position to propose and implement meaningful solutions to problems in a community are those who are struggling the most—regardless of what those coming from the outside might think.

The technical meaning of *relocate* suggests moving from one place to another. In the parlance of the CCDA, *relocation* is typically understood to mean moving from a safe, comfortable, convenient suburban environment to a struggling, impoverished urban area. At the beginnings of the movement, however, the emphasis on relocation had little if anything to do with outsiders moving into poor communities, whether urban or rural. It had mostly to do with challenging people who had left (some would say "escaped") their native communities to return (relocate) to their roots.

In their early days of ministry, John and Vera Mae spent a lot of time and energy investing in people—developing young Christian leaders, helping them hone their skills and abilities through high school and college—only to see them leave their home community at the first opportunity for a better life elsewhere. This may have been good for the individuals who left, but it defeated the purpose of finding lasting solutions to the problems facing underdeveloped communities; their most treasured resources, namely devoted and talented Christian leaders, were being depleted. John and Vera Mae challenged these young people to come back home to live and lead—to relocate.

Three Approaches to Relocation

Over time the CCDA has come to think of *relocators* alongside two other "r" words: *returners* and *remainers*. "Relocators" refers to people who are not indigenous to the community; "returners" and "remainers," by contrast, *are* indigenous residents.

Returners refers to those people originally envisioned by John and Vera Mae, people who grew up in a community and then left for a time to get an education, develop skills or perhaps start a career. Eventually they *returned* to apply their education and skills for the betterment of their native community.

Remainers refers to those who were at some point presented with opportunities to leave their community and its problems behind. Rather than leaving, they chose to stay and be part of the solution.

Whether someone is a relocater , a returner or a remainer, the key principle is that the person lives—and becomes a part of— the community he or she hopes to see transformed. Regardless of which form it takes, relocation entails desiring for our neighbors and our neighbors' families what we desire for ourselves and our own families. It entails living out the gospel in a way that improves the quality of other people's lives spiritually, physically, socially and emotionally, even as one betters his or her own life. It means, in part, sharing in the suffering and pain of others.

Relocaters have a strong vested interest in improving their community. By relocating, a person seeks to understand clearly the real problems facing the poor and begins a quest for real solutions. To put in another way, relocation transforms the pronouns *you* and *them, yours* and *theirs,* to *we, us* and *ours.*

For example, a family that has relocated (or returned or remained) in a poor community will naturally be concerned about educational opportunities in the community. But their concerns about education will not be limited to the needs of their family; they will rather do everything possible to ensure that all the children of their community get a good education. Having relocation as a value in Christian community development leads to communities of believers who take personal responsibility for the development of their neighborhoods and communities.

The rationale for relocation is captured well by Bob Lupton in his essay in the book *Restoring At-Risk Communities:*

> We are finally beginning to realize that programs do not fix communities. Only neighbors can do that. Urban neighborhoods need vested neighbor-leaders who will organize the taking of playgrounds back from the drug dealers. Needed are new homeowners to repair and restore deteriorated homes. Educated neighbors are needed to revive the PTA and turn the schools back into environments of creative learning. Urban renewal, public safety, and public education initiatives funded and operated from outside the community may have their place. But without the leadership of committed, connected, compassionate neighbors who have a stake in the future of the neighborhood, these programs will have little lasting effect.[3]

Remaining

Remainers, as noted, are those who grew up in a community and never left. We liken the remainers to the biblical remnant, that small percentage of people who never strayed from the right path. They *remained faithful.* In some ways the remainers constitute the most important subset of relocaters, for they are usually the ones who understand their community the most, who know its history and its problems the best, and who have the greatest vested interest in making their communities whole.

Thus ministries that are part of the CCDA strongly encourage people to remain. From the time they are toddlers, we want children to see their community as their permanent home—to treat it like a family, which they would never abandon regardless of conflicts or challenges. When they go off to college, we want them to have no thought of staying away permanently. We want them to see themselves as people who will play leading roles in the transformation we all are seeking.

We want to develop in people what some have labeled a "theology of place," a theology lived in the context of an unconditional commitment to a particular neighborhood or community, just as Jonah in the Old Testament was committed to Nineveh (albeit with a little bit of "persuasion" from almighty God!).

A Daunting but Rewarding Venture

The emphasis on remaining notwithstanding, over the years the CCDA has issued what amounts to an open invitation for people who are not indigenous to communities, but who have gifts and talents and a heart for the poor and disenfranchised, to move into poor communities. Knowing that there can be some rocky times—especially at first—we encourage people to commit to staying in their new location for at least fifteen years. Many over the years have felt called to do so, and the number is growing.

Those who relocate in this way are following in the footsteps of Christ by living out a theology of presence. No longer are they merely coming into town from to time to work on a project. By choosing to relocate, these relocaters *become* the project. They have a vested interest in solving the community's problems because, as mentioned, now the community's problems are *their* problems too.

Over the years we have occasionally seen people relocate to poor communities for the wrong reasons. Perhaps they had hopes of being admired or praised for making a sacrifice. Perhaps they wanted to be idolized or glorified in some way for having all the solutions to a community's problems. Or maybe they viewed relocation as a kind of interesting sociological exercise.

Relocating is not some sociological experiment, however, nor should it be romanticized. Rather, it is a kingdom value that should be pursued with seriousness and humility. Relocaters don't come in with all the answers. Rather we come in with humility, as wounded healers, as people who are ready to walk alongside others in search of answers and who are willing to help in whatever ways we can. Relocaters need to be vulnerable, ready to share openly about our own struggles and problems. This contributes to the goal of becoming one with those we love.

It's possible to relocate our houses but not our lives. If people are not involved in their new community—if they don't really know the people, if they never let their neighbors into their houses and never enter their neighbors' houses, if they are not intimately aware of the issues and struggles with which people are dealing, if they don't share tears of sadness and joy as the community faces failures and success—then they have not truly relocated.

I (Wayne) can vividly recall the first time I truly began to feel a part of my new community. I had parked my van on the street and left town for about a week to visit family and friends back in my hometown in Iowa. I returned to find that the van had been broken into. Nothing was missing, but a window had been smashed, and one of my tires was sitting on the front seat.

As soon as I arrived home, one of the neighbors suggested I call the police. When the policeman arrived, he explained to me that while my van was being broken into, one of my neighbors called the police, who showed up quickly to limit the damage. Not only that, but following the incident my neighbors set up what amounted to a 24/7 neighborhood watch until I returned to make sure no further damage would be done.

It didn't matter to my neighbors that I was a white person in an almost exclusively African American neighborhood. The only thing that mattered was that I was their neighbor; they were committed to looking out for me. It was then I knew that

I wasn't just residing in Lawndale. I had become a part of the Lawndale community.

Not all ministries in the CCDA are equally committed to the principle of relocation. In fact, it's quite common for people to offer their talents and financial resources to communities without relocating geographically. While these talents and resources are greatly appreciated and, if managed well, are rarely counterproductive, they do not represent what we would consider to be the *best practices* of Christian community development. (We hasten to add that the CCDA approach is *a* philosophy of ministry, not *the* philosophy of ministry.)

There are tremendous advantages to living in a community where Christian people know each other, see each other almost every day, work and play together, and worship with and care for one another as they pursue a common mission to build the kingdom of God in their own little corner of the world. Except for one three-year period, Anne and I have lived in the Lawndale community since our marriage in 1977. And during the three years we were away, the suburbs did not seem like home. In most (if not all) suburbs today, the sense of community we experience in Lawndale simply does not exist. We love living in Lawndale; it's our home. When we were ending our three-year break, Anne told me, "I'm ready to go home." We can walk to the homes of people from our church. When someone's in the hospital, they have no trouble finding a helper to look after their children or to address any other need they might have. Our testimony—and the testimony of other "non-indigenous" people who have relocated to Lawndale—is that home is wherever we are invested in not only our own future but the future of our neighbors, and the future of our neighborhood. By that definition, countless people are homeless; by that definition, those of us who have relocated in service to the gospel are simply going home.

I'm Here Because You're Here

By Jonathan Brooks

A kid named Darryl once asked me, "You could be rich now. How come you still work in the 'hood?"

"I don't really want to be rich," I answered. "I'm here because you're here, Darryl."

He just smiled. Exchanges such as this inspire me to show young people that success is not defined by escape.

I returned to Chicago in 2002 to be the youth minister at Canaan Missionary Baptist Church in the Englewood community. I was offered this position for two reasons. First, I had an existing relationship with the teens at the church. I started attending the church in 2000, before becoming the youth pastor. Most of the kids in the youth group were brothers and sisters to my friends growing up. Second, no one else wanted the job. I also volunteered to serve at the Diamond Academy, the church's after-school and summer education program.

At first, our family didn't live in Englewood. I lived with my wife, Micheal, and our children in a middle-class lakefront community on Chicago's south side. It was a nice neighborhood, and many of the youth I worked with looked to me as someone who'd "made it."

I had no fear or concerns about living in Englewood. I had grown up there and never thought of my neighborhood as a dangerous place. That was not the case with Micheal. She grew up in the Chatham section of Chicago, a middle-class African American community. We were both raised to believe that success meant getting an education, having a successful career and living in a nice house in the suburbs or an expensive condo downtown. After college, Micheal didn't want to return to Chicago, let alone move to a struggling community. To do so meant failure.

But in 2005 I was invited to a youth ministry conference where I heard Dr. Michael Matta of World Vision speak about youth-led community transformation. It was one of those rare experiences where it seemed like I was the only person in the room and he was speaking directly to me. I left that conference feeling encouraged and believing that God had called me to live in Englewood, and to empower young people there to transform their community.

With Micheal's mixed feelings about Chicago and the approaching arrival of our second child, I had some doubts as to whether this was the right decision for our family. Frankly, Micheal relocated not because she wanted to or felt called to do so but because she believed that I was listening to God.

I know my perspective might be controversial for many couples in ministry. But as the wife of a pastor, I do not believe that my husband's call is necessarily my call. I know that many people feel that whatever their spouse is called to, they are called to as well. I do not agree. I believe that spouses are responsible for supporting one another in whatever the call of God is in their lives.

I did not relocate to Englewood because I felt we were called to pastor! I relocated because my husband was called, and it is my pleasure as his helpmate to support him in that. The calling on my life is different yet complementary to his, and as I discern the plan of God for my life, my husband supports me as I support him.

One way to have strife in your marriage is to approach relocation with the belief that one spouse's call has more merit than the other's. I recommend open and honest dialogue about your concerns before making decisions, as well as continued dialogue as you live those decisions through.

I have supported Micheal in her calling, and she has supported me, and over the years we've both come to love our community.

Lessons Learned

In 2006 I unexpectedly became the Senior Pastor at Canaan. This gave me the opportunity to teach, preach and live out the principles of Christian community development in front of our congregation. Micheal and I have learned a lot along the way. For one thing, we've learned that relocation is a long-term process. Simply moving into a community does not mean you are practicing Christian community development or even relocation per se.

We spent our first few months in Englewood not being neighborly at all. We went in and out of our house through the garage in the back, rarely speaking to any of our neighbors. We did not take our children to the local park; instead, we'd drive all the way to the lakefront to get to a playground. We had moved physically, but in our minds we felt that we didn't belong, that we were to some extent too good to live here.

A turning point came one evening when we were coming home from the church. As I was about to enter the back door of our house, gunshots rang out. It was so loud it seemed the shooter was right next to us. We were fine, but our next-door neighbors' home had been riddled with bullets. Before long, someone was being taken away in an ambulance.

As we conversed with our neighbors, we learned how much we truly needed each other. For the first time, I understood that we are all the same. Tragedy brought our block together; we promised to look out for one another's families and property.

For her part, Micheal has learned over these past ten years that God will take care of us. She has asked God for specific things so that our family can feel comfortable, and God has met every one of the needs—even quite a few of the desires on her list! Our family has learned that where God gives vision he will also give provision. We have seen our faith increase while watching our ministry grow in spite of difficulties, some of them extreme. Micheal believes it's due to our faithfulness to the call of God, which began with our decision to relocate.

Pleasing God is fulfilling in and of itself. Knowing that we are living in the will of God is the best feeling we could experience. We draw on this in the challenging times when it's hard to imagine going on for another year, sometimes even another minute. But we have also found fulfillment in the long-term relationships we have built. As a pastor I get to walk through life with individuals and to see them grow and mature. I share with them many of their greatest and worst experiences and memories. Living in the community magnifies this aspect of pastoral ministry. Our relationships are not limited to the church; they include all of our neighbors. There is nothing more fulfilling than traveling to attend the college graduation of one of the kids who came through the local community center, hanging out at a Memorial Day barbecue or watching our neighbors' fireworks displays on the fourth of July. These are the moments we love and look forward to consistently. With all of the tough things we experience in life, we realize the necessity of partying and partying often!

Advice for Relocators

Early on in my ministry in Englewood, I looked down on individuals who were doing work in the community but not living there. I placed myself and other pastors living in the community on a pedestal, going so far as limiting whom our church fellowshipped and worked with based on zip code. Although it was not done in a mean-spirited way, this was wrong, and it resulted in my alienating myself from some great people and straining many relationships unnecessarily.

Micheal thinks I'm too tough on myself; she attributes my initial hard-headed approach to an overzealous desire to follow God's directions. In any event, I know I grew tremendously in wisdom from my experiences and my mistakes. I've learned, among other things, to leave it to God to work in other people's lives.

I encourage anyone considering relocating to take the decision very seriously. Even for those who are young and single, and have only themselves to worry about, being a good neighbor in a struggling community is hard and takes work. Many want to participate in community transformation without entering into the pain of the people. Learning comes from completely immersing yourself in a community—living with, learning with, and many times crying and struggling with neighbors. The experience is far from pain-free.

Those who come from a culture or ethnicity different from the community to which they are relocating are well advised to dismiss the goal of transforming anything. Just come to learn. This will be appreciated much more than your efforts to "save the neighborhood." If you come humbly with a willingness to learn, you will find in time that you are making a difference, often without even realizing it.

Living in Englewood is hard. We are reminded almost every day that not all is well in our community. Sometimes the pain outweighs the happiness, but the joy has always outweighed the pain. This joy springs from knowing we are following the call of the Lord and that we have so many wonderful, loving neighbors.

Close with Every Step and Turn

By Jared Onserio

In 2004, I came to Atlanta, Georgia, to attend a CCDA conference. The only first-time delegate from Africa, I met with Coach and shared with him our activities in Kenya through a ministry called Global Hope Care. He listened very closely, and I extended an invitation to him to visit my country.

The following year Coach came to Kenya and trained us in the principles of Christian community development. At the time we had trouble grasping many of the concepts. Part of our struggle could be attributed to differences between American and African culture. Yet we learned enough to be able to embark on a new direction.

In 2006, in keeping with Kenya's legal requirements, I registered CCDA Africa and immediately began a publicity campaign advocating Christian community development as a new approach to ministry to needy communities in Nairobi. This was met with great resistance. It was clear that prayer, patience and God's power would all be required to meet the challenges that stood before us.

At the time I resided in Jamuhuri, a middle-class neighborhood bordering Kibera, the largest slum in Africa. I developed a great interest in applying the Christian community development philosophy and approach in Kibera. But this proved to be much harder than I anticipated. My initial ventures into the slum proved to me that my understanding of these communities was actually quite shallow. Christian leaders and pastors who lived in these slums openly wondered if they were being used by organizations little known to them. They considered Christian community development a foreign ideology, and they perceived me, though a Kenyan, as a foreigner with foreign approaches designed merely to raise money and run away. After two years of working in the slums with existing churches and ministries, the only result was disappointment.

I felt compelled to grasp the challenges and problems that stood as barriers to ministry in Kibera. I had to show that indeed I was one of them, that I was capable of understanding them, and that I was able to walk with them and face the same struggles. So in 2010 I took the bold step of relocating to the Kibera slums, despite the reservations of my wife and two sons.

My wife could not imagine how our family would be able to live in a place without clean flowing water and electricity, a place known for extreme poverty, poor sanitation and hygiene, crime of all sorts, and running battles and tribal tensions amongst different ethnic groups. My wife wondered how she could ever invite her women's group from our church in Jamuhuri to visit her in the slums. My sons, meanwhile, lost their neighborhood friends after our relocation. I did keep them in their old school, but they constantly asked me when we could return to Jamuhuri to live.

In short, my family had trouble understanding the call that led to this drastic change in our lives. They begged for explanations, as did my friends, some of whom cut ties with me. Yet I found myself getting deeper and deeper into the slum lifestyle. I gained satisfaction as I started building real working groups, among whom there was profound trust. The suspicion the Christian leaders and pastors had cast on me started to melt away. I found it amazing to realize how quickly a community builds confidence and shares its issues once they see that you are close to them with every step and turn. What made the difference was living among them and listening.

Not everyone was convinced, however. Some of the church leaders with whom I sought to work still did not trust me or what I was doing. They mobilized others against my intervention, claiming that I was using them for my own personal gain. They held parallel meetings to mine, some of which would go late into the night, to discredit my ministry work and motives.

I struggled with this situation for many months until Coach came to Kenya again in 2011 to visit with Kibera pastors. He emphasized leadership that was based on the eight principles of Christian community development, and his words greatly touched many. In 2012 things began to go much more smoothly for my ministry, especially when a big team of students came with Coach to Kibera. People began to see that the ministry I was pursuing had no ulterior motives; we were genuinely trying to help people in need and to build the kingdom of God.

With Coach's 2012 visit, a foundation was laid, and despite the opposition of a few, some fifteen different ministry networks were united into one. After a needs assessment, we determined that tops on the list would be leadership training and micro-finance (offering loans). We chose these priorities partly so that Christian leaders in Kibera can pursue a better education.

There is much to be done in Kibera, but we have come a long way. And the turning point was relocation, without which little if any progress would have been possible. My wife, Mary, and our boys are doing better; they now have a better understanding about how living in the Kibera slum is helping us share the good news of Jesus Christ and do Christian community development.

5

RECONCILIATION

None of the eight key components of Christian Community Development lies closer to the center of the gospel message than reconciliation. In fact, one could make the case that if the entire message of the gospel could be captured in a single word, that word would be *reconciliation.*

Within the CCDA, we pursue three related but distinct forms of reconciliation: people with God, people with other people, and people groups with other people groups.

In Genesis 3 we see that what had been a perfect relationship with God was fractured when human beings ate the forbidden fruit. The rest of the Bible is the story of God's initiative to restore this relationship, with Jesus' sacrificial death on the cross becoming the focal point of human history and of God's plan for redeeming humanity. Paul writes in 2 Corinthians 5:17-19:

> Therefore, if anyone is in Christ, the new creation has come: The old has gone, the new is here! All this is from God, who reconciled us to himself through Christ and gave us the ministry of reconciliation: that God was reconciling the world to himself in Christ, not counting people's sins against them.

Community development is content to help people find a job or a decent place to live. But *Christian* community development includes guiding people toward a reconciled relationship with God through Christ. Evangelism—sharing the message that a right relationship with God comes through Jesus Christ—is central to CCDA ministry. Those who come to know Christ as Savior and Lord embark on a brand new direction in life, a direction that includes freedom from the guilt of past mistakes, a commitment to learn and abide by scriptural principles and a desire to grow closer to Christ with each passing day. In other words, Christian discipleship is central to the CCDA philosophy.

People with People

Among the things that make Christian community development distinctive, however, is the conviction that reconciling people with God is virtually inseparable from efforts to reconcile people with other people. The relationship between people and God is fractured in Genesis 3, but just one chapter later, the relationship between and among human beings is fractured when Cain kills Abel. Cain asks, "Am I my brother's keeper?" The clearly implied answer is, "Yes."

When Jesus was asked by a teacher of the law what is the greatest commandment, he could not have been more clear in his reply. He answered with two commands: "Love the Lord your God with all your heart and with all your soul and with all your mind" and "Love your neighbor as yourself" (Matthew 22:37-39). These commands are inseparable. And when Jesus was asked to define *neighbor*, he didn't say that neighbors are those friendly folks who live nearby or those people we like to hang out with. Rather, he spoke of Jews and Samaritans, sworn enemies of that day (Luke 10:25-37). My (Coach) book *Who Is My Neighbor?* goes into further detail on this topic.

Clearly the gospel demands that we reconcile with those who are different, who are "other," including people whom culture and history have conspired to define as enemies. We question whether a gospel that seeks reconciliation with God without seeking reconciliation between and among others can be the true gospel of Jesus Christ.

The Lord's Prayer suggests that God's kingdom on earth should reflect the kingdom of heaven, which will bring people of every nation and every tongue together to worship Christ. While the Bible transcends culture and race, the church is still having a hard time living out the vision of unity in Christ. Unfortunately, the church has at times in its history tolerated and even promoted unjust and dehumanizing social structures. For example, instead of decrying the caste system in India as an anathema to God, some missionaries were content to establish one church for one caste and a different church for another caste. In the United States the church is, by and large, still divided along racial and ethnic lines. It's true that cultural differences account for some of the separation, but these cultural differences are largely attributable to the evils of the past. We have squandered the opportunity to witness to the world by displaying unity based on love for Christ and neighbor.

Addressing this problem must include acknowledging—collectively and as individuals—that we have a race problem. The original European settlers of North America forcefully took land that had been occupied by other people, reducing the Native American population from 25 million to about 2 million. Over time, the promises made to Native Americans turned empty, as treaty after treaty was broken.

Early Americans also stole untold millions of men and women from Africa over a period encompassing nearly four centuries. Much of the nation's economy was built on slave labor. Some Christians spoke out against the evil of slavery, but most remained silent; others who claimed to be Christ-followers actually developed a theological rationale to justify the practice. It's telling that the United States has never formally apologized for its treatment of Native Americans and natives of the African continent. The U.S. Congress has passed on the opportunity to say, "We're sorry."

We can be grateful for the Emancipation Proclamation, for the abolition of slavery and for the social progress resulting from the civil rights movement. But to conclude that the United States no longer has a race problem is both simplistic and naïve. It's naïve to think that people who for generations viewed themselves as inferior because they were told as much by their government and social convention didn't transfer these feelings to the current generation. Wealth gained through immoral means has largely (though not exclusively) remained in the hands of those who control society. The disproportionate number of African American and Native American people who are poor is a result of centuries of slavery and unjust laws.

Meanwhile, there are people alive today who still remember their fathers, uncles, cousins or brothers getting lynched by white mobs. John lost a brother as a result of a racial incident, and John himself was beaten badly for standing up for basic human rights. Thankfully, we've moved beyond such blatant acts of racism. But even today the illegality of race-based discrimination doesn't prevent social attitudes and public policies from being slanted against ethnic minorities.

That being said, it would be unfair to blame all the problems facing African American communities on white people. Responsible African American leaders, while not dismissing the effects of racism on the past and present, consistently urge people to take responsibility for their own lives—to pursue a good education, to be willing to work for a living, and to be faithful spouses and responsible, caring parents. We all have work to do.

Pursuing Reconciliation

People-with-people reconciliation is greatly enhanced by relocation. The two go hand in hand. When people, motivated by faith in Christ, are living in the same community and working together in pursuit of the same goals, differences are more likely to fade to insignificance. This is partly why the world of sports has led the way in terms of racial reconciliation. When the only goal is to win a championship, the ability to hit a curve ball or make a three-point shot trumps all concern about the color of a person's skin.

Yet reconciliation will not happen automatically just because people live and work together. People, even Christian people, routinely harbor misleading stereotypes and inaccurate perceptions about those who are culturally and ethnically different. This affects everything from how we treat people on an informal basis, to social attitudes, to positions on public policy. Overcoming the obstacles that prevent us from truly knowing other persons requires intentional effort.

Reconciliation in the context of the US church is of course not only a black and white issue. People of many different cultures and ethnicities now live, work and worship in close proximity, especially in urban areas, presenting significant opportunities to be a witness for Christian unity. Reconciliation happens when people are open to listening to one another and to changing their attitudes and beliefs. As we listen to other people's stories and get to know their hopes and concerns for the present and future, we begin to identify one another's deepest felt needs—those hurts and longings that bring opportunities to connect with people on a deeper level, which is always necessary for true reconciliation.

When we listen to other people, we will not always agree with their perceptions. In fact, some of what they say will make us angry. That's part of the process. The goal of reconciliation is not to persuade or be persuaded, but rather to understand and to be understood and respected. The more we understand and respect across lines of culture and ethnicity, the more we will be able to bring together people of all races and cultures into the one worshiping body of Christ and to develop the communities in which we live.

Reconciliation is impossible without a willingness to request forgiveness and to forgive. If we say we have no sin, we deceive ourselves, and the only way to get rid of the influence of sin in our lives is through God's forgiveness. Forgiveness is not a normal or natural act. God intervenes as we forgive one another. In 1970 after being beaten in Brandon Jail, John chose forgiveness over hatred and revenge. Seeds of reconciliation were planted that day, and they have been coming to fruition ever since. John's reputation as a reconciler has taken him to places around the world, including Jordan and South Africa, where he has promoted reconciliation among people groups, efforts that must begin with reconciliation among individual people.

The Only Cure

Ultimately, reconciliation is the only cure for the violence that has its roots in people who are different from one another. Whether it's tribal conflict in Africa, ethnic tension in Europe, the Arab-Israeli conflict in the Middle East, or tension between cultural groups who live in the same community, peaceful solutions start with reconciliation. Reconciliation lies at the heart of peacemaking and living peacefully with one another. Whereas many people groups are concerned about the purity of blood-lines that separate "us" from "them," for Christians the only blood that matters is the blood of Jesus Christ, through which we are all united.

Standing Between Worlds

By Sami DiPasquale

Much of my life journey has revolved around trying to understand and reach out to the stranger, the outsider. In large part I am motivated to do so because in several of the places I've landed, I *was* the stranger, the outsider.

I was born in the country of Jordan to American parents of mainly Anglo descent. Unlike many foreigners in the Middle East who opted to associate primarily with other expatriates, my parents enrolled us children in Jordanian schools. Our family attended a local church, and we lived in neighborhoods where we were usually the only non-Arabs. I spoke English at home, but pretty much everywhere else I spoke Arabic. Almost all my close friends were Jordanians or Palestinians. People who didn't know me often assumed I was a fair-skinned Arab. I had the feeling of not fully belonging or identifying with one specific group of people, except for a small minority known as "third culture" kids—people who belong ethnically to one culture but grow up in a different one. Third-culture kids end up forming a distinct culture that mixes both cultures they grew up in. I am drawn to multiple traditions and feel comfortable many places, but truthfully it's sometimes hard for me to know where "home" is and what heritage to claim.

Ironically, it was when visiting America that I felt more out of place. As a child, I knew little about the United States. I even took English as a Second Language when we lived in Philadelphia for a year because my reading and writing in English were not up to par. My family had little money, but my childhood was rich in many other ways. I was forced by circumstance to learn very early on how to navigate between different cultures, languages and socio-economic groups. I learned how to make friends with people very different from me. I learned that what individuals value the most changes from place to place and from group to group, even among devout Christians.

I learned how deeply family, experience and culture affect our outlook on life, our interpretation of the gospel and what we consider important. I was baffled as a child at how respected Christian leaders in the West placed such a high value on physical welfare, on individual safety and on making sure they were prepared for the future. This was foreign to the reality I had experienced and to my understanding of the Bible. For example, we knew one family of five who lived in their VW van in Amman for weeks or months on end waiting for lulls in the civil war in Lebanon so they could return to their home in Beirut. Another friend about my age seemed to be in shock when his family visited us; he would sometimes have to stay for days in bomb shelters because his neighborhood in Beirut was getting shelled. Many of the kids I played soccer with in the streets and alleys of my neighborhood couldn't afford decent shoes or clothes. This seemed normal to me. People lived by faith day to day, accepting both blessings and hardships. Life was fragile; safety was not considered a foundational human right. It wasn't hard to imagine a suffering Christ choosing to love and forgive in the midst of pain and turmoil.

When visiting America, I found myself wondering how a church elder could occupy an entire dinner conversation in his large and beautiful house with talk about the challenges of the stock market and maintaining a clean swimming pool. Didn't he realize that people were starving, being tortured and having a hard time finding clean drinking water? Did being American, affluent, educated and respected by his subdivision peers give him the authority to speak in superior tones about what Christ *really* meant when he talked about taking care of the poor or living as the birds of the fields? Why did it seem like those who had everything they needed and more clung to their possessions tightly while some of my friends and neighbors in Jordan who had so little were willing to share without regret their torn up soccer ball or little bit of food?

These were the kinds of questions that ran through my head as a kid moving back and forth between the Middle East and North America. As I was entering my senior year of high school my family moved to the Chicago area, and I experienced what might have been the biggest culture shock of my life. We lived in the suburbs and attended a large, wealthy evangelical church. The entire area seemed homogeneous to me—almost entirely white with a healthy respect for order, cleanliness, education, a good work ethic and adherence to the law. I sensed that it was more important to follow the accepted religious and social norms than to answer real questions or embody the gospel, especially when it came to radically loving neighbors, particularly those at the margins.

Life seemed sterile. Struggles were hidden. Streets and homes were perfectly landscaped. Nothing was dirty; older cars could not be seen. Coming from the outside it appeared that everyone said the right things at the right times, dressed the right way, had similar political views and put on a good show of modeling evangelical middle-class Christianity. The rules of this culture seemed to be a moral imperative, and yet these same rules could so easily exclude people of a different culture, ethnicity or socioeconomic status—regardless of the depth of their faith.

I had a hard time reconciling the faith I'd developed over the years with faith as it was now being expressed around me. I had experienced many changes to the rules of the game in my lifetime and had adapted accordingly, but I couldn't muster the desire to adapt to the rules of this game.

After graduating high school, I enrolled at Wheaton College. I was dealing with spiritual questions and struggles that I presume I would have experienced regardless of the circumstances. But over time I grew increasingly bitter toward the white middle-class evangelical church. It felt to me like the reality within this bubble too easily became the moral lens with which to view the entire world, even though the setting was disconnected from the reality in most of the world or even from many places in the United States. I left Wheaton and the United States after my sophomore year and spent a couple of years studying, traveling and volunteering in Egypt and India. I was haunted by my own demons and by my anger and frustration with the church, and a few years later I returned, somewhat reluctantly, to Wheaton College.

This ended up being a time of healing and reconciliation for me. I began to let go of the bitterness I had developed toward mainstream evangelical Christianity and organized religion. There were still many things I disagreed with or felt frustrated by, but I was slowly able to address them in more productive ways, looking for growth rather than division. I was able to recognize and appreciate the beauty that was present, and I was also much more willing to separate individuals from the larger system.

Since graduating from college I've worked for the last twelve years in refugee and immigrant communities in the Chicago area and on the US–Mexico border in El Paso, Texas. One recurring aspect of my work has involved challenging the middle-class church to love and reconcile with its neighbors, particularly those in need or those who are strangers. During this time I've come a long way myself in reconciling with the church. Rather than spending my time complaining about what the church isn't doing, I've tried—however imperfectly—to do something about it.

I've been humbled by the diversity of people God has chosen to accomplish his will (some of whom I may not have chosen myself). I've been learning how to communicate, build strong friendships and love people in the context of the broader church, the very church I once resented. Some of my most joyful moments have come from seeing people from very different backgrounds develop deep relationships with one another—sharing their lives, shedding resentments and advocating on one another's behalf. Witnessing these moments has greatly aided my ongoing effort to reconcile with the mainstream church.

My experience has spurred in me a desire to be an agent of reconciliation wherever I find myself—whether with Palestinian friends in Jordan, with privileged children in Cyprus or India, with orphans and undocumented immigrants in Egypt, with refugees and foreigners or with the middle-class evangelical church in America. Though it can be very difficult and frustrating at times, I feel called to stand between worlds in pursuit of reconciliation.

I've slowly come to realize, whether I like it or not, some of what my national and ethnic heritage bring to the table. Although I grew up as a minority in a foreign country, I am still a white American. And both of these attributes (being white and being American) inherently bring with them a degree of privilege and power. I struggle still to identify fully with this part of myself, yet I feel the need to understand whatever responsibility comes with this inheritance.

From the perspective of my white American heritage, I feel burdened to challenge my brothers and sisters like me to realize some of the implications of being born into the majority culture of one of the richest and most powerful political and social forces the world has ever seen. It is far too easy to remain blind to the pain of those suffering on the fringes of American society, or on the fringes of our globalized world. It can be far too easy to sit back and partake of the benefits of religious, political, cultural, economic and social systems that work so well for us, easy to want to protect the status quo, to blend it with our faith, perhaps even to the extent of demonizing those who question or attack it.

Yet we desperately need to enter into the reality of those for whom our systems don't work—those at the margins, people in run-down inner cities, immigrants looking for work, people in prison, the original inhabitants of this land forgotten on reservations, and those held captive to poverty or oppression around the world, often as a result of US policies. It's impossible for those in power to move toward reconciliation if we are not aware of who we are and of the forces that have formed us and continue to form us. We need to recognize our implicit connection to immoral and unjust actions that have taken place through our history, actions that we may still perpetuate in some way. Listening to the voices and entering into the pain of those on the fringes may indeed be the path to our deliverance.

It's hard for those in power to understand what reality is like for those outside their spheres. Maybe that's one reason why Jesus said it's hard for the rich to enter the kingdom of God. It is so very hard to willingly give up wealth, power, comfort and safety. But that is what our faith requires of us. To that end, we desperately need the friendships and stories that come from the fringes to help us recognize our own poverty, pride and God-complexes.

For people of privilege, reconciliation begins with sinking to our knees before God. We can choose to build relationships with those outside traditional power structures, with people who are "other." We can listen to their stories, paying careful attention especially when we hear a pattern emerging. We can put ourselves under the authority of someone from a different cultural heritage. We can choose to live in a setting where we are the minority. We can study history and theology from the perspectives of those who were not invited into the process of creating the standard textbooks—history can sound so different based on who is telling the story. We can grieve the tragedies that our forebears were a part of and try to figure out how they factor in to how we live today. We must ask God and others for forgiveness, and we must forgive ourselves. Finally, we must move forward, always listening, always striving to embrace voices from the outside with a resolve to confront the sin of injustice at every opportunity.

I envision a time when God will make all things whole. But in the meantime, we are invited to participate in the coming of the kingdom by becoming agents of reconciliation *today*. May God give us the courage to make the sacrifices that will be asked of us.

6

REDISTRIBUTION

Along with relocation and reconciliation, redistribution is one of John's original "Three Rs." But as with *relocation,* the word *redistribution* carries with it some unintended and misleading connotations.

To be specific, *redistribution* is commonly associated with economic socialism—taking from the rich and giving to the poor until income has been divided equally among all. In fact, this has nothing to do with how redistribution is defined and understood within the CCDA.

The CCDA as an organization functions apolitically. That is, it takes no stand on political issues, and its understanding of and approach to redistribution (despite the word's connotations) are completely consistent with capitalist economic philosophy.

The CCDA's theology of redistribution begins with an affirmation of Psalm 24:1:

> The earth is the LORD's, and everything in it,
> the world, and all who live in it.

The Bible teaches that we are not owners but rather stewards of all the gifts, blessings and resources God has given us. In many places throughout Scripture, we are instructed to share our resources to help those who are less fortunate. We read in Acts 4:32: "All the believers were one in heart and mind. No one claimed that any of their possessions was their own, but they shared everything they had." Paul instructs the Philippians, "Don't look out only for your own interests, but take an interest in others, too" (Philippians 2:4 NLT). These verses have nothing to do with government-mandated sharing or "redistribution" as typically understood. They speak to sharing that is motivated by love for others and by a desire to abide by scriptural principles.

The CCDA recognizes that sharing with others can be complicated. If we are not careful in how we share, we can wind up hurting people rather than helping them. For their own good, people need to do their part—to help themselves as they are able—so that they won't always be dependent on others, and also in order to reach a point where they too can experience the joy of helping others. For example, in the Old Testament, Boaz didn't give Ruth a handout; he gave her an opportunity to work. She didn't have any land, so Boaz generously allowed her to work on his land. Ruth did the work.

This has long been the approach of ministries in the CCDA and of groups such as the home-building ministry Habitat for Humanity. In accordance with Habitat's philosophy, if people are able, they are expected to work alongside the volunteers who've come to help them build their new home. Some call it "sweat equity." It helps to develop in people a sense of pride in ownership.

Striving for Justice

The CCDA's approach to redistribution focuses not on income but rather on opportunity. This includes creating economic opportunity for people. We recognize that people will do different things with the opportunities they have. Some will make better choices than others. But everyone ought to have a fair opportunity for the good things in life, and the plain truth is that in our culture and in cultures around the world they do not. The playing field is not level. Regardless of the society, those in control tend to make laws and establish policies that consider their own best interests over the interests of others—especially the poor, who are often voiceless and disenfranchised.

Consider this: one person can make a mistake in judgment and steal something worth a hundred dollars or less, spend some time in jail (thus paying their debt to society) and then have trouble finding a job for the rest of their life. Meanwhile a white-collar worker who deprives hundreds of people of thousands of dollars can declare bankruptcy, and in seven years all is forgotten.

Or consider this: why is it that the overwhelming majority of drug abusers are young white men, while the overwhelming majority of those who are in prison for drug-related offenses are young black men?[4]

Redistribution for the CCDA means, in part, striving for justice—especially in underserved communities. It means working to bring justice to our criminal courts and prison system, to hiring practices and housing policies, to the educational system. We need to work to change laws, policies and attitudes that give some people unfair advantages over others. Justice should not be available only to those with the economic means to acquire it. Redistribution cannot be separated from efforts to pursue social justice.

Education as an Equalizer

One could easily make the case that the single most important avenue for creating fair opportunity is education. Education is the great equalizer, a major pathway to redistribution. No matter the socioeconomic starting point, if someone is given the tools that come from learning, he or she has the opportunity—the fighting chance—to get to a different place. In this age of technology, it's especially important to make sure that children and youth gain the computer skills they will need to compete in today's world.

And yet to say that public schools in urban communities are substandard is a colossal understatement. In fact, in some school settings it's virtually impossible for students to learn.

It's not fair to place all the blame on schools or teachers. As anyone who has taught in an urban public school knows, the challenges are multifaceted. For one thing, it's very difficult for teachers to succeed when so many of the children they're trying to help come from broken homes or uncaring families.

Regardless of who is to blame, ministries in the CCDA are addressing the challenge of the education gap through initiatives such as after-school tutoring and remedial summer educational programs. Some ministries also do their best to make it more financially possible for young people to go to college. As schools have deteriorated in poor communities, it's now very important to bring back good, quality education so that the poor in America can have a chance to flourish.

Redistribution Through Microenterprise

Another way the CCDA pursues redistribution is through economic development—identifying needs for goods and services and then starting or supporting businesses that will meet those needs. For anyone still concerned about the connotations of the word *redistribution*, this kind of activity represents capitalism at its best.

When I (John) was eleven years old, I worked all day hauling hay for a white man, and he gave me fifteen cents. Even at a young age, I could see that those who worked the hardest and those who profited the most were usually not the same people. It all came down to who owned or controlled the means of production. The man I worked for owned the mule, the wagon and the field. It was a microcosm of the difference that exists between the "haves" and the "have-nots." We've all heard the saying that if we give people a fish, they'll eat for a day; if we teach them to fish they'll eat for a lifetime. Redistribution CCDA-style goes further by asking a question I raised in my book *Beyond Charity*: Who owns the pond?

In valuing redistribution we support efforts that enable people from poor communities to own bigger and better ponds. We do this by assessing the community's needs and the skills that are available to address those needs in ways that are financially profitable. Underserved communities are not completed deprived of wealth, and we have found that people of limited means will pay for goods and services that scratch where they are itching the most. In pursuing redistribution we don't underestimate people's ability to make good choices with their limited resources. The goal is to make more and more good choices available to them.

Ministries in the CCDA are attempting to change disparity between the haves and the have-nots through supporting microenterprise—helping entrepreneurs start businesses that not only meet the needs of the community but that also improve the economy of the community. This happens when businesses are based in the community; money made by those businesses is recycled within the community as opposed to exiting to some other place.

Microenterprise is not easy work. Often, something that seemed like a good idea for a business turns out to be not so good once the market has its say. Some businesses will fail. But even when this happens, there is something to be learned.

In developing locally owned businesses, we should make it a priority to keep as many jobs as possible within the community. If people don't have the necessary training or skills, we should think about how we can provide training to develop the required skills. This is what we did with the Lawndale Christian Health Center. We realized that many of the positions that were needed to provide quality health care could be filled by people from within the community. They had the desire and the aptitude. All we had to do was train them.

In sum, redistribution for Christian community development ministries is about creating fair opportunities for people to live healthy and fulfilled lives. It includes providing better opportunities for quality education. It entails harnessing the commitment, energy and resources of men, women and young people living in the community, the commitment and energy of community residents is as much an asset to be redistributed as financial resources; young people whose energies are going to gang activity, or whose talents are being directed toward work that could never develop the local community (e.g., sports, the arts) might be channeled toward a different, community-directed end (e.g., arts education, coaching), as well as of outsiders—employers and others—who care about the community and who want to contribute their knowledge and resources. It means finding creative avenues to develop jobs, educational programs, health centers, home ownership opportunities and other enterprises that support long-term economic and community development. It will often include advocating for public policies that are fair and just, that level the playing field of opportunity. All of this taken together constitutes redistribution CCDA style.

Redistribution, Exchange and Kingdom Stewardship

By Bob Lupton

Most fundamentally, redistribution in Christian community development is about people sharing their lives with others in ways that bridge the chasms of class, race and culture. Coupled with relocation and reconciliation, redistribution is the natural outcome of being a neighbor in a diverse community. It is neither a doctrine nor a formula. It is a predictable result of engaging in authentic relationships with those who are different from you.

In fact, *exchange* might be a better word to describe what we mean by redistribution (except that it doesn't begin with R!). "Exchange" assumes that everyone has something of value to contribute to the life of a community. No one is so broken, so dysfunctional, so disadvantaged that he or she has nothing to offer. The key is actually believing this to be the case, then identifying and engaging the talents that reside within each of our neighbors.

It doesn't matter, for example, that my next-door neighbors are gay. What is important is that they keep an eye on my house when I am out of town. When my car won't start in the morning, I call my mechanic neighbor, no matter his race or economic status. When my child has a fever and upset stomach, my neighbor who is a nurse is the first person I phone, regardless of her religious affiliation. Even the men who hang out around the fire barrel outside our thrift store add value to our community; their watchful eyes provide a measure of security.

And then, of course, I myself have certain resources that are of value to my neighbors—tools to lend, contacts that can lead to employment, a computer for homework assignments. Because we live in proximity to one another—and because we must depend on one another (for safety if nothing else)—the opportunities for exchange become a normal part of community living. Exchange as a community value is motivated at least by self-interest, if not also by more noble spiritual values.

Such sharing of talents and resources is more common among the poor than among the affluent, for sharing becomes essential for survival when resources are scarce. Those with abundance have less need for others. In mixed-income neighborhoods this difference can prove problematic. Virgil, my neighbor who lives in a volunteer-built house across the street, shared with me one day about the struggle he and his wife, Tamara, experience as they stand in the rain at the bus stop in the morning and watch my wife, Peggy, and me drive past in our separate cars. It's hard, he has said, to see neighbors who have so much when his family has so little.

"Would it be better to live in separate communities where we are not confronted every day with these inequities?" I asked him.

"Oh no," Virgil responded emphatically. "This is our spiritual work—to not be envious!" The benefits to his family living in a healthy mixed-income neighborhood, Virgil says, far outweigh the struggles.

My spiritual work, I have to confess, has been learning to share. I grew up in a family and a culture where self-sufficiency was the normative value. There was little need for sharing. As a matter of fact, it was considered inappropriate to borrow from a neighbor. Every family was responsible for addressing its own needs.

Even among our family members, each of us had our own room, our own clothes and our own "stuff." You didn't get into someone else's things, at least not without permission. So when I relocated to a mixed-income neighborhood, I was not at all prepared to freely lend my lawn mower and my tools—let alone my car (never!)—to neighbors, for whom sharing was an expected practice.

Though I had been taught all my life about stewardship, it had always been interpreted in terms of being responsible for the things

God had entrusted to my care. That interpretation actually makes it quite difficult to distinguish stewardship from ownership. The idea of letting go, of allowing others to share in the use and responsibility of my material assets, was as foreign to my thinking as reconciliation and relocation.

The morning I watched Virgil and Tamara pull away from my house in my late model Chevy on their way to the coast for a long-delayed honeymoon (with their kids!), however, I experienced a momentous internal value shift. It was a shift from individual ownership to kingdom stewardship. My possessions, I realized in a very vivid way, were not my own. This shift in values has proved not to be a one-time event; I've learned that this "spiritual work" of letting go of personal ownership appears to be a lifelong process.

Redistribution is not one-way charity. No country on earth responds more generously to victims of calamity and times of crisis than the United States. It is part of our national character that we can be justifiably proud of. But most of the needs of the inner city are a function of chronic poverty, not crisis. And chronic need calls not for crisis intervention but for a development response. When we attempt to address a chronic need with an emergency response, the results are seldom positive.

In the context of chronic need, redistribution that is essentially one-way, crisis-oriented giving often yields unintended consequences. It can foster beggary. And a loss of dignity. And unhealthy dependency. And an eroded work ethic. And dishonest relationships. One-way giving is the opposite of mutual exchange; it subtly communicates that the recipient has nothing of value to offer the giver. Reciprocity, on the other hand, is based not on the giver or the recipient but on the relationship; it assumes that both parties have something of worth to contribute to the other. Thus redemptive redistribution—redistribution according to the values of Christian community development—must be a two-way street.

7

LEADERSHIP DEVELOPMENT

During his time on earth, Jesus fulfilled many roles, among them the roles of prophet, teacher and, of course, his primary purpose: to sacrifice his life for the salvation of humankind. But sometimes we in the church focus so much on Jesus' mission as Savior that we don't pay enough attention to the many practical lessons he taught and modeled—lessons that ought to guide the efforts of Christian community development ministries in their efforts to develop leaders.

In our 2012 book *Leadership Revolution*, we devote two entire chapters to Jesus' approach to leadership and leadership development. Most of the content in these chapters was derived simply from examining the Gospels, with a focus on studying Jesus as a leader and developer of leaders. We point out, among other things, that Jesus was proactive and intentional in choosing the people who would eventually become leaders of the early church. He was accessible to those he was developing. He spent lots of time with them, including quality time. He took advantage of opportunities to teach people the things they needed to know in order to become leaders. He modeled authenticity by sharing with his disciples his vulnerability—his pain, his fear and, sometimes, his frustration and anger. Far from putting on an act, Jesus "kept it real."

Among the ways Jesus prepared leaders was by giving them assignments. When they did things well, he was quick to affirm them. And when they messed up he did not hesitate to set them straight. Because those Jesus was developing were completely secure in his love for them and his devotion to them, Jesus could be totally honest, completely candid. He didn't have to worry about walking on eggshells with them.

While Jesus was quick to correct and admonish, he never gave up on people. He was willing to give those he was developing second and third chances, more if needed. Peter is an excellent example of this (see John 21).

Finally, and perhaps most importantly, Jesus modeled humility. His entire purpose as a leader was rooted in serving others as opposed to rising to the top of some organizational chart. He said to his apostles, "Whoever wants to become great among you must be your servant" (Matthew 20:26). In Matthew 23:12 we find Jesus saying that "whoever exalts himself will be humbled, and whoever humbles himself will be exalted" (NIV 1984). And this to his followers: "Whoever wants to be first must be slave of all. For even the Son of Man did not come to be served, but to serve" (Mark 10:44-45).

Filling the Leadership Void

The void of leadership is among the most significant characteristics of struggling communities. In many urban communities, leadership—defined in terms of having influence—is confined mostly to the church and to drug dealers. Thus the church, invested in building up the community, is in constant competition with leaders whose influence works to destroy communities by feeding the related pathologies of addiction and crime.

Many of those who reside in inner-city communities can remember a time when there was not such a dearth of leadership. Children had role models not just in their homes or on television but in their communities. They witnessed adults going off to work each day. Neighbors would stop children on the street and, for all the right reasons, ask to see their report cards. Many people felt a responsibility for *all* children, not just their own. Contrast that with today's reality wherein so many children and youth barely have a relationship with their parents, let alone other adults in the community. Far too many fathers have left the scene, some because they're serving time in prison.

The absence of strong leaders is both a cause and an effect of urban decay. As inner-city communities began to decline, those capable of exerting a positive influence began to leave. As they did, conditions worsened, and even more of the communities' best and brightest took flight. This classic "downward spiral" has been well documented in numerous sources. For many, "success" came to be defined in terms of escaping the inner city in pursuit of a better life. This escapism defines success as owning a home in a more affluent community; it has drained urban communities of the resource most needed to solve their problems—in a word, *leadership.*

This dearth of leadership and its contribution to declining communities is not limited to cities. Many areas of the United States have been witness to the suburbanization of poverty. The response is the same: people leave, and they don't come back.

At least in urban areas, people have access to public transportation so they can get to the city center and have access to shopping, restaurants, entertainment and more. Some suburban areas, by contrast, have declined to a point where they are fortunate to have a post office. People living in impoverished outlying areas have no easy way to access the goods and services they need. Thus, developing leaders has become one of the CCDA's eight key components. The primary goal of leadership development is to restore this much-needed stabilizing glue to communities, thus filling the vacuum of moral, spiritual and economic leadership that is so prevalent in poor communities. We aspire to redefine success for people not in terms of escape but rather in terms of leadership.

The leadership development component of Christian community development is thus closely related to the concept of relocation, because the most effective way to accomplish the goal of developing leaders to raise up Christian leaders from *within* the community of need. Those who come from the community—who deeply love it and who consider it their home— are best equipped to know their community's strengths and weaknesses, its problems and, most importantly, the solutions to those problems. By and large, those who have opportunity to leave and yet remain in (or return to) in their home community to live and to lead will prove to be the community's most successful leaders. They are in the best position to create in their communities a nurturing environment saturated with inviting opportunities.

A Long-Term Proposition

When Anne and I (Wayne) began in Lawndale, the importance of developing indigenous leaders wasn't immediately clear to me. A conversation I had early on with the late Tom Skinner proved to be a major turning point in my thinking. I expressed to Tom my frustrations at not being able to find skillful, motivated African American leaders to walk alongside me. I asked Tom where I could find such leaders, convinced that he would steer me in the direction of Howard University, Morehouse College or some other historically black college or university.

Instead, Tom took me by the arm and said, "The reason you can't find the leaders you're looking for is that you're looking in the wrong places. The truth is the best leaders you can find are already here, right here in Lawndale."

He could not have been more right. At the time Tom shared with us this wisdom, some of Lawndale's best and brightest future leaders were only three, four or five years old. Others hadn't even been born. That day, Tom told us that developing indigenous leaders would take consistent effort over a long period of time. He challenged us to commit to remaining in Lawndale for at least fifteen years, for that's how long he thought it would take for indigenous leadership development efforts to begin producing fruit.

In fact, it was thirteen years before our ministry produced its first college graduate who returned to Lawndale. Thirty-eight years in as of this writing, we have seen more than 250 young people from our community graduate from college. About a hundred of them have returned.

Perhaps it's clear by now that developing indigenous leaders means that most Christian community development ministries place a major focus on children and youth. We need to pay special attention to those children and youth who have little or no support from their families. For them, the church needs to become the village they so desperately need.

The goal is to win young people to Christ as early as kindergarten and then to provide them with spiritual and intellectual nurturing all the way through college. So a dynamic youth ministry is a priority; it lies at the heart of making disciples and developing future leaders. We need to do whatever it takes to make sure that our young people don't just tolerate church but find it meaningful and relevant to their struggles and goals. The hope is that after college these young men and women would not even consider "escaping" their community but will come home and do their part to fill the leadership vacuum. The goal is not merely to make Christians of our young people, but to make disciples, as the Lord challenged us in Matthew 28:19.

One way to determine if a church or ministry's commitment to indigenous leadership development is what it ought to be is to examine its priorities in terms of time and resources. Creating a youth-friendly environment will likely require those who've been around for a while to be open to change. They may need to be welcoming of new worship styles and unfamiliar music, for example.

At Lawndale, the youth are one of our top priorities—if not the top one. Anne and I teach Sunday school for high school students and are otherwise very involved with them. When the church celebrated its thirty-fifth anniversary, we could sit back and enjoy the service; the youth planned and led every part of it. Symbolically this said a lot about our priorities. We believe that if children and youth are not the number one expense item, the ministry needs to ask itself how serious it truly is about developing indigenous leadership.

Sadly, there are legal situations that prevent ministries in the CCDA from doing all they might want to do to develop indigenous leaders among youth. For example, some Latinos and people from other ethnic groups are negatively affected by their legal status. Young people are not able to attend college or prepare for a stable career. Therefore, in some cases ministries are moved to engage in social action to challenge immigration laws that debilitate the lives of promising youth and their families. This interest in immigration reform is thus not simply a matter of concern for individuals—although CCDA ministries are concerned with the well-being of individuals in their care. Social action in our communities is part of our long-term investment in our communities; it is part of the way community leadership manifests itself, and in the case of laws that affect youth, it's part of the way a community stewards the leadership gifts of its children over the long haul. Noel, our CEO, has been at the forefront of the immigration discussion nationally.

Everyone a Leader

Leadership development, however, is by no means confined to youth. Leadership guru John Maxwell defines leadership as "influence—nothing more, nothing less." Based on this understanding, no one should ever feel too old or too uneducated or untalented or too (you name it) to lead. Anyone can lead.

That being said, one of the challenges of developing leaders is that not enough people see themselves as having leadership potential. But if leadership is simply a matter of influence, virtually everyone is a leader at some level. Fathers and mothers influence their children. Aunts and uncles influence their nieces and nephews. Someone in an office setting has some measure of influence over coworkers. Even a seven-year-old child has influence over a younger brother or sister. When all people view themselves as leaders, they are more likely to seek opportunities to lead, and they are more likely to prepare themselves for those opportunities.

Pastors from time to time ought to use the pulpit to encourage people to recognize their leadership potential and to challenge people to aspire to greater leadership responsibilities. Several characters from both the Old and New Testaments can serve to illustrate sound leadership principles. Churches and other organizations involved in Christian community development can also make use of formal leadership development programs—as simple as inviting people to take a leadership course, one that includes textbooks, assignments and perhaps a leadership project. (For anyone looking for more specific direction, the CCDA leadership can provide it.)

Those who are developing leaders must recognize the importance of their role as mentors. Jesus taught the masses and had many disciples. But he was especially close to some, namely those he called to be his apostles. And even among those twelve there were a few with whom he was particularly close.

In similar fashion, it's important for leaders who are developing leaders to identify a few in whom to invest in a special way. Mentoring in this way means spending quality time and sharing insight and wisdom at every turn. Many leader developers within the CCDA adhere to the maxim "Don't go anywhere alone." If they're going to a conference or sporting event, they take someone with them. Each minute spent mentoring is an opportunity to develop a future leader.

Consider the Future

A good leader recognizes that the time will come when he or she is no longer around to lead. Thus one of the goals of a good developer of leaders is similar to one of the goals of a good parent: to work oneself out of a job.

Leaders need to view success in terms of what is best for the long-term health and vitality of the context for their leadership, as opposed to what is best for them as individuals. If an organization's efforts fall apart the minute a leader is gone, then that leader did not do what was necessary to assure long-term success.

If a leader is suddenly gone from your ministry, will you be able to carry on without missing a beat? You need to do all you can to make sure the answer is yes. Transferring power and authority to others is not enough. Leaders must also make sure that those others have access to the practical information they will need—everything from keys to the buildings to passwords to the bank accounts. Keeping track of what goes wrong when a leader goes on sabbatical or takes an extended leave of absence is a good way to determine if the ministry is adequately prepared for a leadership transition.

Leadership development flows naturally out of the three Rs—relocation, reconciliation and redistribution. That's because leaders take appropriate responsibility for their place, their relationships and the long-term growth of their community. Because everyone is, to some degree, a leader, then leadership development is a big job! But because everyone is a leader, the developing of other leaders is ultimately everyone's responsibility. And so communities grow as leaders invest themselves in leadership.

Leadership and Shared Life

By "Q" Nellum

Developing leaders requires nothing short of investing in other people—a chosen few—not just for a specified period but for a lifetime. As a "people person," I have always been able to connect with others easily. But I've learned that it takes way more than just being a people person to connect long-term with individuals, to make a difference in their lives and especially to help them develop as leaders.

First and foremost, those in whom you are investing your life need to be reminded regularly that you are there for them. There is something about people knowing that they have somebody in their corner that gives them the strength and confidence to go on, especially when life is difficult. We need to be available to those we choose to disciple, raise up, lead and mentor. They need to know that there is no problem or issue they can't feel completely free to tell us about. There is no time of day or night when my friends can't feel free to call if they need help. This kind of reassurance can happen via text messaging, through social media, by phone or in person.

To state it another way, we need to include those we are developing in our lives and even, at times, in our families. I spend time with the people I lead to help them academically, spiritually, emotionally and with life skills. I take students shopping with me or to the laundromat. I have brought people to my house and taught them to cook. They have taken care of my kids. I lead them in Bible studies. I train them to lead at camps, at their schools and in their homes. I took on the art of listening to the students I lead—learning the lingo of the day, living in their pain with them, celebrating their joys and working through their chaos. I consider it vital to be in every part of their lives somehow, even if this develops a little piece at a time.

Building leaders in many ways begins and ends with relationships. It's about sharing life with others. I am awed by how God has allowed the fruit of new young leaders to emerge after years of my walking with them in life.

Because there is so much involved in the process of leadership development, it is important that you choose people you feel you are called or drawn to for a lifelong investment. Several years ago I met two young girls who were a part of a middle school Bible study at our church. They were quiet; they seemed very shy. They had just committed their lives to Christ through the Bible study. As we exchanged greetings, I felt drawn to these girls, though I didn't quite know why. A year or so later, as they entered high school, I connected with them again and felt strongly that we were destined to stay in each other's lives forever. I didn't know why at the time, but I do now.

At the time our lives began to intersect, I had already been involved in youth ministry for several years. The girls I felt drawn to are twins, though each is unique in personality and character. At the time I met them, they were fairly recent immigrants from Namibia, Africa. I was amazed at the joy they had despite the circumstances in their household. They had grown up with eight siblings, one of whom had passed away as a child, which took a heavy toll on the family. For years their mom, Mae (Portuguese for "Mother"), had been battling schizophrenia and depression. Their dad, an alcoholic who used to beat their mom, left the family, but Mae stayed faithful to him and continued to consult him on decisions affecting the children. Mae had only a fourth-grade education. She received government assistance and took multiple medications to help with her illnesses.

The twins seemed to me to have taken the weight of the family on their shoulders. One of their two older brothers had moved out of the house and wasn't much help; the other was working a lot. So most of the household responsibilities fell on the twins.

Mae would have mental breakdowns and get taken to the hospital, leaving the twins to cook for their younger brother and sister and get them to school. They had to do their homework and help the younger kids with theirs. Their only mode of transportation was the bus. All of this was really rough on the girls, but they valued family and loved their mom so much that they never considered their situation a burden. I admired the girls and their mom because their mom stayed faithful and the twins stayed committed.

The girls exhibited strong moral character. They didn't drink, party or do drugs, and they were committed to remaining virgins. Given the trials in their lives—and the temptations that confront all young people—their behavior seemed almost too good to be true. But these girls had begun to go deeper in their walk with the Lord.

When we invest in the lives of others, we can easily sense when something is wrong. One night after a prayer service, the girls hung around longer than usual, and I felt that God was telling me to ask them what was going on. When I did, they started to cry. Some of the sisters at the church joined me as we gathered around them and prayed for them. The girls told us that Mae had been taken away again to the hospital. They had no money for food. They were tired, worn out from all they were having to do to make it from day to day. And they were scared that this time their mom would not come back home.

The church was there that day to help them to restore some semblance of stability in their lives. When Mae did come back home, she wanted to talk to me. In Portuguese—the language of Namibia, where their family was from—Mae effectively declared her desire to adopt me into their family as her daughter,.

I was honored, and I accepted. After all, the twins and I had spent so much time together I felt like they were my little sisters, and they had always shown great respect for my husband and me. From this moment, we became a family together. It was beautiful and strange all at the same time, but it was right.

Mae still battled her sickness and became really depressed. The twins eventually grew up and left the house. Both received a Daniel's Fund Scholarship—essentially a full ride to the college of their choice. They stayed local and often came home during the week to help their mother and to spend time with her. Their growth spiritually during this time was tremendous. Both helped me lead Arts N' the Hood, the Christian performing arts camp my husband and I run. They had also begun mentoring some of the younger girls. They were doing well, and the family was growing stronger.

It was Father's Day in 2009 when I got a call while I was at church. One of the twins had gone to her mother's house to pick her up for church. She found her mom dead. Mae had committed suicide. I went to the house as quickly as I could. One of the hardest things I have ever had to do was to be there for a family who had just lost their mom.

The siblings looked to me for leadership. Even the older brothers accepted me as the "big sis." All of us stuck together, grieved together, cried together, prayed together, struggled together and just sat in stillness together. Our church rallied around and came daily with meals and prayers and financial help. This brought us all closer together.

Going through Mae's things led to many discoveries and brought back many memories for the children. Through it all, God showed up and was present. But it was hard. The twins, as well as other family members, went to counseling to help them get through. A year later, one of the older brothers took his own life, and we had to come together again as a family.

Over time, the twins became the glue that has held the family together. One of the twins now works with me; the other is a nurse. They are both truly amazing to me, and I continue to look up to them and admire them because they have trusted God enough to bring them through and they continue to trust God to complete the good work he has begun in them.

We build leaders by investing in the lives of others. How do you know that you are supposed to invest in a life for a lifetime? I believe you know when you take time out to listen to God and as he takes you to the people you are supposed to disciple. How this looks can vary, but the key is to build a relationship. Don't be afraid to open up your life as you enter into the life of another. Sharing life is what it takes to develop leaders.

Leadership Development in the 'Hood

By Joe Atkins

At Lawndale Community Church we define *leadership* as influence. Twelve years ago, I moved with my family from one area of North Lawndale to another. Not long after settling in, we were approached by a five-year-old girl whom I'll call "Re-Re." As I approached the front gate of our home, she asked, "Are you all a family? Is that your wife? Are those your kids?"

I could not help but chuckle at this beautiful child's boldness. I replied "yes" to all her questions. To my surprise, she said, "I want a family just like that."

This dialogue made leaders of the Atkins family, for we had influence over this young child.

Developing leaders in my community begins with living my life well. To have a positive influence on others, a person must first die to himself or herself. As Paul put it in Philippians 2:17: "But even if I am being poured out like a drink offering on the sacrifice and service coming from your faith, I am glad and rejoice with all of you."

Living in North Lawndale has not always been easy, as my wife, Stacy, often reminds me. Sometimes the sacrifice seems greater than the pain of the journey. But the truth is we would not have it any other way because we feel called to be a light, to offer hope, to be a model for others. I'm drawn to the message of Matthew 5:16: "In the same way, let your light shine before others, that they may see your good deeds and glorify your Father in heaven." Being a leader meant I had to realize that my life is not my own. It belongs to the Re-Res of North Lawndale.

Hope

Great leaders commit to offering hope to others. It doesn't matter what a community has going for it if it has lost hope: "Hope deferred makes the heart sick, but a longing fulfilled is a tree of life" (Proverbs 13:12).

Leadership is grounded in the Word of God, which offers hope no matter how bad the situation. Romans 12:12 challenges us to be "joyful in hope, patient in affliction, faithful in prayer." Our hope as leaders must be translated into hope for those we are leading and developing as leaders. Many of them come from backgrounds where hope was hard to find. Thus we must "dance our hope" in front of others, sometimes on a daily basis.

I have come to believe that the number one reason people fail at leadership—or resist the opportunity to become leaders—is fear. They fear that others will not follow; they fear they might fail; they fear that people will attack them. And no one can guarantee that these things won't happen. But I like to live with the promise of 1 John 4:18: there is no fear in love; perfect love drives out fear. So if we who are leaders and leader developers are motivated by love, we need not fear, nor should we lose hope when things don't go as we planned or hoped they would. Love drives out fear—the destroyer of hope. And if our hope is rooted in Christ, it will not disappoint (Romans 5:5).

Paul and Onesimus

I identify a lot with Paul's account (in his letter to Philemon) of his relationship with Onesimus. Paul, writing from prison, provides a blueprint for leadership development. He first encounters Onesimus in his holding cell. Lesson one: you never know when or how God will drop someone onto your path. But when it does happen, it's important not to be surprised, for these things happen according to God's plan (Ephesians 1:11).

I met Jerry Bolden in October 1995 in the middle of one of the busiest streets in Chicago. He approached me using my nickname: "Are you JoJo?"

I said yes reluctantly. Because of my history with the drug culture, I thought some people might be looking for me for the wrong reasons. Thank God, Jerry was looking for me for the right reasons. He wanted help from our Hope House ministry, which over the years has helped thousands of men overcome their struggles with addiction and live productive lives. In many ways, Hope House is like a holding cell for the Onesimuses and Jerry Boldens and Joe Atkinses of the world—those who have struggled, who have been discarded or cast away, who have lost hope.

Leaders commit to loving those we are developing, even when doing so is hard. Perfect love offers hope to people, many of whom have been told time and time again that they are no good, that they'll never make it. Paul saw potential in Onesimus. He saw an opportunity to glorify God. He started by loving Onesimus, and eventually he led him to Christ. It all happens quickly in Philemon, but in my sanctified imagination I believe that Onesimus was a bit of a project, that he was not so easy to love. As Paul came alongside Onesimus, so I came alongside Jerry, first to offer the help he needed and eventually to develop him as a leader.

I had to make the practice of patience a priority as I worked with Jerry, but I knew how to do so, because Coach had been so patient in developing me. Like Paul with Onesimus, Coach saw potential in me. When I struggled with drugs, he remained patient. And when I finally overcame my addiction, he walked with me patiently, first on a path to true wellness and eventually to my becoming a leader.

I've learned that leader developers are not enablers. They don't run to the rescue when those they are developing make mistakes and get into messes. They recognize that both positive and negative behaviors come with consequences. Coach allowed me to make my own mistakes and then to work through the consequences. This was the hard part for me, because I wanted him to enter my messes and make everything right. But I have thanked God many times for Coach's wisdom in not rescuing me. He understood that my growth would require accountability and periods of pain. His goal was to build me up. And no matter how many times I failed, he remained patient; he never stopped loving me. He knew he was working with a man who was broken but who had great potential and was open to learning.

Faithful prayer is another key component of leadership development. Building others up to be leaders requires that we spend a lot of time on our knees. I'm sure Paul prayed without ceasing (Ephesians 6:18) for Onesimus. Change likely did not come easy for Onesimus. It certainly did not for me. Coach had to stay on his face for me, and I know he is still on his face for me, faithful in prayer, interceding on my behalf—as are many others.

I have interceded many times for Jerry. He came from a background of drugs, gangs and jail. He was tough when I met him, but Jerry is my heart today, just as I am in Coach's heart. I became Jerry's advocate when he sought employment at Lawndale's health center, and I'm proud to say he has been working there now for twelve years. He has a beautiful wife, two beautiful sons and his own home.

Leadership development is ultimately a gift we pass on. We give what we have received from others. When an Onesimus drops into your life, see it as another opportunity to develop leaders for the kingdom!

8

LISTENING TO THE COMMUNITY

There's something about hearing a person's story. Whenever I (Coach) am alone with someone from our Hope House ministry for people coming out of prison or recovery, I ask them, "Tell me your story." I learn something every time. Sometimes I even learn creative ways of stealing!

All people are created in the image of God. Listening to the people we walk alongside emerges from this understanding. Because of this, they have inherent worth, and so do their thoughts and ideas. They should not be viewed as projects but as people; their lives—including their dreams and ambitions—are as important and valuable as anyone else's.

A community's residents comprise the vested treasures of its future. Unfortunately, this understanding does not always come naturally to people from underserved communities, who often struggle to recognize their own full humanity and self-worth. Listening to people affirms their inherent dignity. It demonstrates a theology based in humility.

When Jesus was going through Samaria and met a woman at the well, he listened, and then he met her at her point of need. Listening was his starting place for addressing what the woman,

whether or not she realized it, needed most: life-giving water
from the stream that would never run dry.

Listening to the community includes listening to individuals
in the community. It should be considered a daily event. Elderly
people love to tell their stories, and often people who have
struggled in life want to share with others the challenges they
have faced. So we listen—traveling with others to a conference
or event, pairing up on a work project or talking at social gatherings, we take the opportunity to listen. When we invite people
to tell us their stories, it shows that we care.

As an act of caring, listening can be viewed as an end in itself.
People will bring up problems and challenges, and we won't
always have answers. That's okay. In fact, we have learned over
our years in ministry to be skeptical of those leaders or aspiring
leaders who think or say they have all the answers. It's those
who realize there are no easy answers who usually are the most
successful. Simply listening is, in its own way, an answer; for
again, it shows that we care.

Avoiding Paternalism

Listening to the community emerged as a key component in the
CCDA in part to combat a paternalistic approach to solving a
community's problems. We define *paternalism* in terms of outsiders—usually people who have achieved some measure of
success in the eyes of the world—coming into a community
and communicating, in their approach and general attitude,
"We are successful. We have the answers. We know what works
and what doesn't work. Just listen to us, and eventually everything will be fine."

One of the potential side effects of such a paternalistic approach is that it causes people in the community, who most need
to participate in building the community, to step aside. They

think they have nothing to contribute because someone else can do it better. They then never have the opportunity to grow in their skills and, more important, in their self-confidence.

Development workers overseas, pure as their motives might be, have made this mistake consistently over the years. Perhaps, for example, US workers can do a better job building buildings than Haitian construction workers. But if US workers swoop in, take over and do it all, they effectively put a fledgling Haitian construction company out of business, thus helping to make the country permanently dependent. This all too common dynamic is aptly reflected in the words "unintended consequences."

However, our emphasis on listening to the community goes far beyond simply allowing indigenous people the freedom to fail so they can learn and grow from their mistakes. We have learned through experience that, more often than not, those who are the most deeply rooted in their community understand their community and its nuances and complexities most completely. Thus, even though they may lack the resources required to put their proposals in place, they generally have the best ideas for solving their problems.

Not long after I (Wayne) moved to Lawndale in 1975, I learned a lesson about listening to the people, a lesson I've never forgotten. It's a story I've told many times over the years. We were discussing the community's most immediate needs at a gathering. I already knew the answer though: I had grand visions of building athletic facilities or a health center. The people, on the other hand, simply wanted a safe place nearby to do their laundry. They wanted a washer and dryer.

I said to them, "Let's pray about it." The people didn't realize at the time that "Let's pray about it" was my way of saying, "I don't want to do it," so they took me seriously. They began praying for a washer and dryer.

Sure enough, not long afterward we got a call from a family in the suburbs whose mint condition washer and dryer no longer matched the color scheme of their house. Word had spread about our fledgling ministry, and these people wanted to make a donation.

I politely explained that, despite our gratitude, we had no way to transport the washer and dryer to our location. Much to my chagrin, they told me that they had access to a pickup truck; they would gladly make the delivery.

Suffice it to say that the washer and dryer served our community faithfully for several years. More importantly, I learned a lesson about listening to the people. We didn't have the funds for my grand vision; meanwhile God granted the prayers of my neighbors. I learned that the community knew better than I what they needed the most and what they could realistically acquire.

I wasn't the only one who learned something. The people of Lawndale learned that the leaders of our church were willing to listen to their ideas and do what *they* thought was important versus what *we* thought was important. In essence, we began earning the trust of the people by listening.

Listening to the people leads to participation by the people. This is true of everyone, not just those who live in struggling inner-city communities. Over the years, the CCDA has learned that not only do the people with the problems usually have the best solutions for solving their problems, but they are also far more likely to take ownership of their own ideas and proposals than they are of the proposals and ideas of others. And also far more likely to work to make their plans succeed.

Asset-Based Community Development

CCDA ministries have increasingly taken an approach to listening popularized by John McKnight and Jody Kretzmann, co-founders of the Asset-Based Community Development Institute, located at Northwestern University's School of Education and Social Policy. In contrast to grant-providing foundations, which typically want to hear about a community's needs, McKnight and Kretzmann focus on a community's assets—its resources.

Highlighting needs can lead to people feeling overwhelmed. It risks tearing people down, which understandably chips away at community morale. In keeping with McKnight and Kretzmann, we recommend making a list of the community's assets: What are the positive things it has going for it?

No asset is too small or insignificant. There is an older woman in Lawndale, for example, who every morning spends more than an hour with a broom cleaning up all four corners of an intersection where drug dealers hang out each night and deposit their litter. Doing this each day clearly establishes that this woman cares about her community; she is a huge asset.

At some point, of course, the discussion must turn to *applying* the community's assets to its needs. With this in mind, we recommend yearly community listening meetings. These meetings include twenty or so residents who are not part of the organizing church or ministry. Guided by an indigenous leader, these meetings aim to identify four or five areas of struggle in the community and identify at least a preliminary plan for addressing each of them. The plan should include the presence of community stakeholders throughout the process.

It's important to focus on things that can be done right away. Many ideas get nipped in the proverbial bud because they require a grant, and getting grant money takes time, and success is never guaranteed. Pursuing grants is, in most cases, a good thing to do, but it should not stop us from asking, "What can we do right now with what we have?"

It's important for people in the community to understand how much more we can accomplish if we work together—how much greater the whole can be than the sum of its parts. The children's story "Stone Soup" illustrates this point well. Two men come to a town looking for something to eat. The only thing they have with them is an empty cooking pot. No one is willing to share any food, so the men find a stream and fill their pot with water. Then they drop in a large stone and begin heating the pot over a fire.

When curious passersby ask what they're doing, the men talk about how delicious their stone soup will be when it's finally done. But it needs a little garnish, just a few spices. This is not too much to ask, so one of the villagers complies. Then the men say the soup would be perfect if only someone could spare a few carrots. Another villager complies. Then it's onions and potatoes and other vegetables. Finally comes the meat. The story ends with everyone in the village enjoying a delicious and nourishing pot of soup, all because they put their resources together.

In sum, listening to the community enables us to build relationships and to uncover the qualities, talents and abilities the community has to address and eventually solve its problems. Listening helps community members to see themselves—not some government program or outside group—as the source of answers. It is essential for leaders to help the community focus on maximizing its strengths and abilities in order to make a difference. The CCDA philosophy, rooted in the conviction that the people with the problems have the best solutions, affirms the dignity of individuals and encourages the community to identify and use its own resources and assets to bring about sustainable change.

Coming to Understand

By Jember Teferra

In 1974, a Marxist military revolution came to Ethiopia. My husband, a government official, was among the first twenty-five political prisoners to be taken. I was expecting my fourth child, so this was obviously a very difficult time.

After two years of looking after my husband in prison and struggling as a single parent caring for my four children, in 1976 I became a political prisoner myself. At the time of my arrest, I honestly could not relate to the prisoners I knew from the Scriptures—Joseph, Paul or our Lord himself. I found no joy, contentment or sense of purpose in my suffering. Instead, I felt angry at God, and I had no desire to accept my fate as part of God's plan.

Little did I know how much what I learned in prison would serve me later on in ministry.

For one thing, I learned that I could not simply impose my values on other prisoners, including my fellow political prisoners. My approach and advice were frequently rejected, which taught me the importance of having the right attitude and of listening. I learned out of necessity to be a facilitator instead of an imposer of my viewpoint.

Second, I came to understand more closely what life was like for the poorest of the poor. Most of those in prison had committed crimes motivated in large part by their poverty. I witnessed what life was like for people who lived day-to-day, hand-to-mouth. It was easy for them to succumb to fatalism and apathy. I had the opportunity to reflect on the relationship between crime and poverty and on the whole spectrum of social justice. I also learned the importance of extending Christian forgiveness—leading to healing and reconciliation—in order to serve God.

In 1981, after five years in prison, I was miraculously released. I felt better prepared, better groomed for the tasks and the mission that lay ahead. Soon after my release I was offered many fancy jobs (I suspect out of sympathy for what I had been through), including some high-salary positions with the United Nations. At the time I recalled having a dream at the age of ten in which I felt challenged to work with the poor. I had another vivid dream now, calling me again to work among the poor. Ultimately I started the Integrated Holistic Approach Urban Development Project. I still look back in wonder at how the Lord calls his followers to different ministries. I now believe, from my own experience, that the call we receive from God is loud, clear and persistent.

Everything I learned from my prison experience, including the need for bottom-up approaches to addressing poverty, was rooted in Christian values.

Among them was an attitude of humble listening, which leads us to respect the poor among whom we are working, to regard them as dignified participants in their progress, not merely as subjects upon whom we can impose our will and carry out our plans. Nowhere in the Gospels does our Lord impose his will on others. He invites his disciples to follow. The disciples voluntarily sacrifice whatever ambitions they may have had in order to do so.

I also learned that ministry is *with,* not *for.* It begins with listening to the voices of the target community *with* whom (not *for* whom) any development work should be planned and implemented. Development workers are enablers and facilitators, not dictators or imposers. They recognize the target communities as owners and sustainers of their own programs who shoulder the responsibility and gradually take on full leadership. As a handbook for urban ministry operations I recommend the book of Nehemiah, the tale of a humble leader who worked with the people to rebuild Jerusalem.

For ministry in difficult situations to be successful, everyone has to be on board, pulling together in the same direction. Everyone's perspective must be taken into consideration. When this happens, people's entire lives are focused on the ministry goals. There are no standard working hours; rather, working hours arise as a response to demand. In my case, not only my mother and husband but also my children and some of our extended families have been helping to support and enable my work. We who are part of the Integrated Holistic Approach Urban Development Project live out the culture and philosophy of the project daily. We eat together, pray together, mourn together and celebrate together. Each of us has had to struggle at times to sacrifice professional identity and supposed expertise for the sake of the family, the team. This is one of the things that happen when we are committed to listening.

This empowering, wholistic approach to ministry—humble listening, enabling and facilitating, family and team identity—is, unfortunately, popular in theory but difficult in practice. Most secular and some Christian donors see this approach as too costly and time-intensive. However, God has enabled us to overcome this reluctance and has led donors to support our approach and our work, in some cases despite their reservations.

Today, in the original four *kebeles* (neighborhoods) where we became active, people from the community are running the show. A community-based board has been established. The people feel empowered. They have regained their dignity and, with the help of capacity building and skill training, manage their own development program.

Urban ministry is difficult. It will not be everyone's calling. But it is mine. Whatever our individual calling, each of us should strive to bring the good news of Jesus Christ whenever and wherever we can, promoting social justice and alleviating poverty in our limited spheres, wherever they may be. As we do so, we must not underestimate the importance of listening.

The Process of Finding Solutions

By Scott Lundeen

According to the CCDA philosophy, the people with the problems have the best solutions for solving their problems. I must confess that over the years I've struggled with this assertion. Quite honestly, I'm not always so sure I believe that the people with the problem really do have the best solutions.

I can't help but think of Sara, a teenager left sobbing on the street after being ditched by a middle-aged man following a private tryst. Neighbors stood and watched; her mom came to scream at her. I think I know a better way to parent than that.

At community meetings, I've seen neighbors lament gentrification, but they have no national context or perspective on the issue. I'm different: I've got information that can help. I've got solutions!

I've seen leaders who no longer live in the neighborhood rehearse the same plans and ideas they've been talking about (but not implementing) for fifteen years. Not me—I've got follow-through solutions!

I've seen new neighbors run meetings with barely concealed disdain for the poor folks who don't share their middle-class values. Compare that to me: I've got solutions based on the CCDA's core values.

I'm just full of solutions! Perhaps my exceptional insight into solutions was best on display after Hurricane Katrina. Our family lived in a low-income, African American neighborhood in New Orleans. We evacuated the city in the middle of the night—some thirty hours before the storm hit. Our church pulled together about seventy people, many of whom did not have an easy way to get out of the city or a place to go. We headed to Jackson, where John Perkins met us in the middle of the night and made breakfast for us in the morning.

Our section of New Orleans was comprised of more than 80

percent renters. Two-thirds of our neighborhood experienced flooding. Because of a connection with an international relief organization, a few of us were able to get back into the city within a week. We were saddened by what we encountered—a flooded, dark city patrolled by the military. We heard many a tragic story from friends and neighbors.

I dreamed of solutions. Filled as I was with ideas I had learned through the years at CCDA events, I envisioned a different neighborhood. Not different neighbors, but better schools, more home ownership, renovated housing projects. We flew in some CCDA board members to get their perspective, but I knew what we needed to do. Our church needed to buy up lots of property. I made a connection with a local real estate agent to research and prepared to make purchases. Lots of them.

As the weeks went by, we began partnerships with schools associated with the Knowledge Is Power Program (KIPP), and I connected with a very gifted young developer who had done some major nonprofit development work in Atlanta. We began to develop a strategic plan for our neighborhood.

We partnered with a couple of national organizations (including Habitat for Humanity) to get hundreds of homes cleaned out, remodeled or built. But this represented only a tiny fraction of our neighborhood. Some new charter schools were birthed in the area, in part because of the investment of a committed coworker, but mostly because of other influences and only after years of work. We bought three properties—including a fourplex that utterly consumed us. There were structural issues, major problems with donated materials, and significant violence and drug traffic on the block.

Today, I cringe just thinking about it. Prior to Katrina our church had focused on youth outreach. Real estate and housing were not our strengths. The plan we'd put together was an affront to the work of the local neighborhood association, and it never gained any traction. I'm not even sure where the documents are now. Some major government and private development muscle renovated most of the three local housing projects. Local businesses have been birthed and have partnered to see other changes. We made some meaningful progress in schools. But in many ways the neighborhood still feels the way it did ten years ago.

For good reasons and with good will, I left the community two and a half years after the storm. Most of my bold ideas passed away, and the church is back to doing the things it does best: pastoring and developing youth. So much for my great solutions.

I was introduced to the values of the CCDA during my college years. My class visited the Lawndale neighborhood and met Coach in January 1992. Over the years I went back often. I've been to a Farragut–Collins high school basketball game, attended a Dynamic Twins concert with the Lawndale youth group, attended church services in the gym and at another facility, and eaten a few times at Lou Malnatti's in Lawndale. I've attended a bunch of CCDA conferences and workshops, and I have built friendships with people implementing CCDA ideas around the country. Maybe that's why I thought I had solutions. I've seen "best practices," and I'm quite sure some communities where I've lived and worked haven't been using them. If only they would start a jobs program, a lending group, a development association, an advocacy network . . . I could go on and on.

As I reflected on my life, I realized that I didn't even have solutions for my own problems. I mean, I didn't know much about choosing a college or being a good husband or dad or creating videos or investing money or managing people. I needed other people to give me their solutions to those challenges.

Then it hit me like a boulder. The best solutions—even the "best-practice" solutions from others—never sank in for me until I was ready for them. And even then, they had to be tweaked and contextualized. I was always impressed by the great leaders with solutions—from CCDA board members, to authors of books about leadership and contextualized theology, to friends and acquaintances who knew how to manage time and money and family. But I assimilated these ideas at my own pace. And the people who exerted the most influence over my decisions were the men and women whom I considered my leaders—men and women who listened to me, asked questions, made suggestions and supported me when I took a risk.

I've learned that Christian community development work is as much about the *process* of finding solutions as it is about the solutions themselves. It's the same in my life. One listening leader in my life invited me back to Denver after New Orleans, and with his encouragement I launched a video series designed to engage leaders in urban issues and CCDA values. The series brought me across the country to interview both well-known and little-known community members and ministry practitioners. I listened to them and then worked to craft video stories that communicated the things I learned while sitting and interviewing in parks, churches, living rooms and community centers. In a very concrete and real way, listening to the community became my work. And my specific job was to broadcast the stories—not so that other people would fix things but so they would listen.

It's tempting for me to think that the job creation initiatives in North Carolina, the housing development work in Atlanta or the medical facilities in Chicago that I've come to discover in these videos are the solutions. In reality, the solution is sitting with someone in a living room and listening to their dreams, experiences and ideas. The next step—whether a washing machine, a business or simply another cup of coffee—will emerge when it's ready.

Ministry starts with listening. By asking questions, you build a relationship, and you hear felt needs. The longer you listen, the more you come to understand unique concerns, needs, hopes, gifts and contexts. You also build trust. Along the way, you will begin to recognize and affirm solutions as they present themselves.

Our ministry in Denver has developed a relationship with a group of extraordinary women, most them retired from white-collar jobs. These women have an astounding array of gifts and international connections. They are a local expression of an international relief organization, and each year they choose a few projects to join with. Our residential college student leadership program is one of their projects, and for a couple of years, that's how we felt: like one of their projects. Our students stood to learn a lot from these women, but our young people weren't always receptive. At one social event, a student was given a winter coat and came back saying, "They think we're homeless!"

These women wanted to come once a month to serve a meal or tutor. They had done this in other settings and offered it to us. They had a lot of experience and many solutions, but they were not taking the time to listen. Fundamentally, we came to realize, we didn't need what they were offering. We could live without this group. But what our city needed was friendships. Our city needed a twenty-four-year-old Latino DJ to be friends with a retired white executive.

So now our meetings with these women are explorations in mutuality. We talk about websites, social media, science or human trafficking. At one especially poignant meeting, our topic was simply "lessons learned through failure." Everyone shared a story of pain or failure and how God worked in it. We were all a little stunned at the stories we heard—surprised at the honesty and the struggle we shared, despite our differences.

Our relationships are changing; there is new openness. Instead of coming with coats or dinners, these remarkable suburban women are coming to listen. And an equally remarkable group of young urban leaders, open to their friendship, are listening too. In the process, some real solutions—very different from coats and dinners— are being shared on both sides.

Listening to the Community 115

I'm reminded that my growth—and the growth of any individual or community with a problem—will not result from a solution but from a process. A process that starts with listening to the community.

Allowing the Community to Be the Guide

By Patty Prasada-Rao

"Listening to the Community," as the CCDA understands it, is about more than just being a good listener. It's about deciding that what someone else has to say has meaning for what you do, how you do it, when and why you do it, and for whom you do it. It is allowing the community to be the guide.

Listening to the community doesn't happen by default. It takes both intentionality and humility. It requires paying attention so you can recognize when you are not listening. It means realizing that when you instinctively think your own ways of doing things are better, you inadvertently communicate that other voices do not have value. Listening asks you to be quiet and to hear not just with your ears but also with your eyes, your heart and your soul. It asks you to pay attention to what others are saying (or not saying) with their mouths and also with their actions, their pain, their songs, their lives.

Listening Lessons

I'm a "certified talker" and off-the-chart extrovert, but I also care deeply about people, and I understand that listening is a way to show that you care. I learned to listen early in life. I was fascinated by the stories my parents told of growing up in India. I got a glimpse from these stories that sometimes well-meaning people of God do things in a way that might hurt the people they think they are helping.

Western missionaries to India shared much of their lives and love with my family and their communities. But structures, systems, economics, traditions and even theology at times resulted in a two-tiered level of community life. Some stories sadly revealed a lack of respect for local customs and values if they contradicted the Western, "Christian" way of doing things.

There were also, however, wonderful stories of loving relationships between Western missionaries and the local Indians, along with amazing opportunities of empowerment and leadership development for many in my family. Those are the stories that stuck with me, shaping what I thought I would eventually do. I wanted a career where I could live with people in mutual love and respect, and together make life better for everyone.

I've learned over the years to pay attention to the voices that were not the loudest, the ones that needed an invitation to speak, for great wisdom has often come from those who thought they didn't have much to say. As a staff member with InterVarsity Christian Fellowship at Loyola College of Maryland, I found myself learning from a mixed group of Protestant and Catholic students. The IVCF chapter at this Jesuit campus had been seen as the Protestant student group, while campus ministry events were for Catholic students. Catholic students involved in the Fellowship helped me understand what it felt like when other students questioned their faith because they were Catholic. Together we worked hard to help each other listen, and we began to understand that Protestant students didn't own the label "Christian." We pushed beyond our preconceived notions of what it meant to follow Jesus by listening to each other, and as a result we drew closer in community and ministry.

Listening well usually happens best in the context of relationships. I was introduced to the CCDA while leading IVCF student interns in the Baltimore Urban Program. They were immersed in living, worshiping and working with an inner-city church's summer youth camp. The director of the camp was a white woman (Joan) who worked with two full-time African American staff (Denise and Jocelyn). All three had known one another other for some time.

The interns met weekly with the church's pastor to share the history of the neighborhood and church, and to provide training in the philosophy of Christian community development. Because of their close relationship with Joan, Denise and Jocelyn shared their disappointment at not being included in the sessions with the interns. They felt they were being left out. I'm sure this was not the intention; perhaps the objective was not to overload them with yet another meeting. Nevertheless, when Joan shared their concern with the pastor and me, and we gladly welcomed them to join us. A richness came from this time for the interns, for they heard not only the pastor explaining the philosophy but examples from community residents about how these principles were lived out. But it took the strong relationship between Joan and Denise and Jocelyn, the freedom they had to speak honestly with each other, to bring that rich experience about.

Listening well takes time. Individuals are more likely to engage in their own neighborhood when their voices are heard. When our local Habitat chapter was planning their first project in new housing construction, the development of twenty-seven row homes, they gathered neighborhood residents to help determine everything from the inside layout of the rooms to the front stoops, to sidewalks out front instead of grass. Residents even offered help on how to deal with rats—something nonresidents would not have thought about!

When you're trying to help a community, you can think you are doing something that makes sense based on your background, but it may not be the right thing for the context you are in. While helping with our school in my grandfather's village in India, I noticed that delinquent school fees were often addressed by either punishing the students publicly during assembly or asking the cycle rickshaw driver to tell the parents as he dropped off their children. This didn't seem respectful to me, so I suggested writing notes to send home with students. My cousin, the principal, declined to implement this plan, and the situation repeated itself the following month. I again suggested we try this more discreet way of notification. We tried my idea the next month.

Within a few days, I heard an angry parent talking with my cousin. I asked him what this was about, and he said the parent wondered why we had disrespected the family by sending a note home about school fees instead of just asking the rickshaw driver to tell them. Apparently written notices were reserved for something legal; our note made the parent feel like a criminal.

I learned two things: (1) I didn't always know the best way to do things, and (2) my cousin might not feel comfortable telling me my ideas were not so good. It was incumbent upon me to invite feedback. I learned that when an idea I presented wasn't incorporated, it usually meant my American way needed some Indian adjustments!

Listening well means being willing to own your stuff and to confront some of what might not be pretty. One of the greatest privileges of my life was to serve as co-executive director of New Song Urban Ministries with Antoine Bennett, a lifelong neighborhood resident and community leader in Sandtown. I had the academic training and world credentials; he had the heart, love and respect of the community. In our five years together, I learned that my ideas for New Song's programs were only as good as my willingness to let them be shaped by Antoine's wisdom and perspective. It was hard at times, when I thought my sixteen years in Sandtown had given me a good perspective on things, to hear him say, "Patty, you need to understand . . ." But it was also an honor to hear him say, "I know you love Sandtown, and I'd have you speak on our behalf anytime."

Listening to the community is key in the work we do together. What a privilege it is to draw close as we come to know another person's heart, to be welcomed into what a community values, to share dreams for what we want our neighborhood to be, to find our place in helping make that happen. When we listen and are listened to, we know we are valued, affirmed, seen for who we are, appreciated for what we bring. Listening helps us understand that we belong to each other and to God.

9

BEING CHURCH-BASED

The church—followers of Christ gathered as a community—is God's chosen change agent for ministry. The church consists of people, and of course all people are flawed. But imperfect though it is and always will be this side of heaven, the church is nevertheless the blueprint God has ordained for his people to gather as a worshiping community and to minister and witness to the world.

The scriptural evidence is strong in support of this conclusion. In Matthew 16, Jesus cites Simon Peter's recognition that Jesus is "the Christ, the Son of the living God" as "the rock" on which our Lord would build his church, against which the gates of Hades will not prevail. Paul writes that the mystery of Christ

> has now been revealed by the Spirit to God's holy apostles and prophets. This mystery is that through the gospel the Gentiles are heirs together with Israel, members together of one body, and sharers together in the promise in Christ Jesus. (Ephesians 3:5-6)

Paul declares his mission to "make plain to everyone the administration of this mystery, which for ages past was kept hidden in God, who created all things." And then he delivers the clincher:

> [God's] intent was that now, through the church, the man-
> ifold wisdom of God should be made known to the rulers
> and authorities in the heavenly realms, according to his
> eternal purpose that he accomplished in Christ Jesus our
> Lord. (Ephesians 3:9-11)

We love the church. I (Wayne) love being a pastor of a local church. The people of Lawndale Community Church help me understand the Christian life much more deeply and power-fully. Anne and I would not still be in Lawndale were it not for the gracious and loving people of Lawndale Community Church. One could make the case that it is the church that separates *Christian* community development from community development.

The CCDA's principle of being church-based overlaps with other key ministry principles, most notably the commitment to wholistic ministry. In his (highly recommended) essay "The Local Church and Christian Community Development" in the book *Restoring At-Risk Communities,* Glen Kehrein wrote, "A rudderless ship would easily go astray. The local church acts like a spiritual rudder for CCD ministry."[5] Glen passed away in 2011. He was a CCDA founding board member and the founder and executive director of Circle Urban Ministries in Chicago. He was an innovator and a critical thinker who understood that it is virtually impossible to carry out effective wholistic ministry apart from the local church. A nurturing community of faith can best provide the thrusts of evangelism, discipleship, spir-itual accountability and relationships through which disciples grow in their walk with God.

Kehrein links the church—the faith community—with the

principle of reconciliation. It makes sense to do so, for reconciliation entails forgiving and asking for forgiveness. It's about healing relationships, and it's the church—not an organization, not even a parachurch organization—that is most dedicated to building, sustaining and healing relationships. As Kehrein puts it, "Solid ministry grows from solid relationships and the church provides the opportunity to develop those solid relationships."[6]

In a similar vein Mary Nelson, the retired founder and CEO of Bethel New Life in Chicago, often says that the church is "the gas, the guts, and the glue" that holds the community development ministries of Bethel New Life Church in Chicago together. The gas provides the energy, the guts provide the core purpose, and the glue keeps everyone on track, moving in the same direction.

Reclaiming Responsibility

The community of God's people—the church—is uniquely capable of affirming the dignity of the poor, which includes providing people with the skills and opportunities they need to meet their own needs. One can easily make the case that the reason so many parachurch organizations came into existence is that the local church was not doing its job. We can be thankful that parachurch groups have to some degree stood in the gap left by the church even as we regret that this was necessary. If, for example, local churches in college towns were conducting Bible studies, discipling young people, sharing the gospel and meeting the needs of college-age youth, there would be no clear mission for organizations such as InterVarsity Christian Fellowship and Campus Crusade for Christ.

The church has routinely been either an absentee or an unfriendly neighbor in communities across our country. By posting

"No Parking" and "No Trespassing" signs and keeping their doors locked except for Sunday mornings and maybe Wednesday nights, churches have passed on opportunities to serve their communities and thus to build the kingdom. They've become virtually irrelevant with respect to addressing the needs of the people around them.

The CCDA challenges churches to reclaim their responsibility to minister to their communities—most centrally in community development. The church's responsibility is not limited to activities associated with Christian spirituality such as evangelism, discipleship and spiritual nurturing. From the command of Jesus, it is also the responsibility of churches to love and serve their neighbors and their neighborhoods. This understanding of the role of the church is present throughout the New Testament, including in Acts and the Pauline epistles (see, for example, Acts 4).

Reclaiming responsibility might entail developing relationships with parachurch organizations that are doing the work of loving their neighbors. In this way, parachurch ministries can at least be connected with—if not under the authority of—the local church. The CCDA also encourages churches to work together to accomplish common goals. Lawndale Community Church has worked with as many as twenty other churches on initiatives that will benefit the Lawndale community. For example, a coalition of churches in Lawndale, along with the Lawndale Community Development Association, built multisite affordable housing on the site where Martin Luther King lived for a short time in 1966. We called them the Martin Luther King Legacy Apartments.

The Parish Concept

At the center of the CCDA's commitment to church-based ministry is an emphasis on parish. It's a wonderful thing for a church to support overseas missionaries or efforts and initiatives that have worldwide implications. But these should be never eclipse caring for the people in the church and loving and ministering to those in its "parish"—that is, in the neighborhood or community where the church is located.

Churches need to view themselves not as a collection of individuals but as one body whose parts work in concert in pursuit of common goals. This one body is characterized by a deep love for all the body's parts, as suggested by Paul: "If one part suffers, every part suffers with it; if one part is honored, every part rejoices with it" (1 Corinthians 12:26).

The parish concept, among other things, takes seriously the African proverb, "It takes a whole village to raise a child." There was a time when communities, including urban communities, functioned in significant ways as villages. People looked out for one another. If a child was headed in the wrong direction, neighbors made sure the parents found out about it. But today there are virtually no villages left in our society. The NIMBY effect ("Not in my back yard") is a contributing factor—people don't feel a responsibility to the community they're in, and consequently churches wind up being commuter-friendly rather than community-friendly.

The local church has the opportunity to become a village, to be a place of supportive community to people from birth all the way to adulthood. Churches can be places wherein children are assured of getting gifts at Christmas and are remembered on their birthdays. They can be places that support people who need help with childcare, who are looking for jobs or who want to go to college. Such is the vision behind the parish concept.

Staying Grounded

The CCDA has about a thousand member organizations. Only a small percentage of these are churches, but most are connected in some way with a local church. Ideally, all of them would be. Without this connection, it's easy for a community development ministry—despite its faith-based roots—to drift away from its biblical, theological and spiritual moorings, much the same way so many colleges that were planted by churches have evolved into secular institutions. The local church provides the moral authority and spiritual direction ministries need to stay grounded and on track.

It often happens that community development ministries outgrow the church that oversees them. A church of only eighty to a hundred members might oversee housing or health care ministries with hundreds of employees and with budgets that dwarf the church's budget. It doesn't matter how big these ministries get, so long as they operate under the umbrella (and thus the moral authority) of the church.

Typically church members serve on the governing boards of the various community development ministries. It's conceivable for a person to operate under another person's authority in the community development ministry workplace but to exercise authority over that same person in the context of the church. This can be—and usually is—a very good thing, because it results in a kind of mutual accountability. It can also be "sticky" and "messy," but it forces people to come together and work out their differences.

At Lawndale we have intentionally entangled the church with community development ministries. The church owns the buildings that house the development corporation, legal center and health center. The boards are interlocking, which means we have to sit down and talk and, if necessary, work out differences.

Perhaps most significantly, because community development ministry is about building and sustaining community, it belongs under the authority of a local church. Ultimately, building community is a central mission of the local church. The church is the place where people who have relocated geographically find friendships and grounding in their new environment. It's where local people can practice hospitality—welcoming the stranger in their midst—and experience deliverance from the isolating and dehumanizing forces of contemporary culture. It's the place where people can find people with whom they can worship and share their lives—both their joys and their burdens. Young people don't stay in a youth group or high school or college forever. They don't have the same doctor all their lives. But the church family—the body of Christ—is there for people from birth to death, through all the passages of life. It is unique in that regard.

Furthermore, while so many communities are divided by income, class, ethnicity, social stature or some other segregating principle, the church serves as a major force for unity. As a microcosm of God's kingdom, the church welcomes everyone—people of all ethnicities, rich and poor, strong and weak, powerful and powerless. A worshiping church breaks down the barriers that divide people in communities. It helps people understand that every single person has gifts and talents to be used for the greater good of the community and the body of Christ. How exciting it is to see doctors at a local health center worshiping alongside their patients on a Sunday morning, property managers worshiping with their tenants, teachers worshiping with their students, police officers and firefighters worshiping with their neighbors. This is community building at its best.

A Parish Mindset

By Thurman Williams

New Song Community Church (NSCC) is "a multi-cultural community-based church committed to loving God and loving our neighbors in our Sandtown community by ministering comprehensively through a church-based Christian community development model." This is our mission statement. We list the eight key components of Christian community development in our church bulletin each week; for us, the church is the foundation from which our other programs emanate, programs such as Sandtown Habitat for Humanity, our New Song Community Learning Center and New Song Family Health services. While the church's relationship with these entities looks different now than it did when we began them, it's still the case that we see them as tangible expressions of the church's ministry in the Sandtown neighborhood of West Baltimore City.

We begin each year in New Song's worship services with a sermon series on the eight key components of Christian community development. We do this to help explain our philosophy of ministry to newer folks and to remind older members of how we're living out who we are. One of the things I say is that Christian community development is not just a tack-on to the ministry of the church or the concern of only a focused few. Rather, it is a philosophy that permeates everything we do: what I preach on, who's up front during worship, our leadership structure, how we do our budget and more. Our church is not just a chaplaincy for the community-development ministries; it's where the ministries began and where the programs remaining under the church's leadership receive their direction, support, influence and accountability.

During the annual sermon series I typically preach on Jeremiah 29:4-14, which is a portion of Jeremiah's letter to the Jewish exiles in Babylon. In the context of that letter, Jeremiah proposes two negative options regarding the exiles' posture toward Babylon. The first option—isolation—is put forth by the false prophets. They defy God's Word to them and tell the people they should not invest in the city; they won't be there long, so they should be ready to leave as quickly as possible.

The second option—assimilation—is promoted by the Babylonians themselves. They wanted the Israelites to just blend in and become like them. It was a brilliant strategy because, if effective, it would mean that the Jewish culture would be wiped out after a generation.

But the call to God's people through the prophet Jeremiah was not to isolation or assimilation, but rather to *transformation*. They were called to be salt and light in the place where God put them. God called them not to withdraw from the city but to seek its peace and prosperity (*shalom*), for in the city's peace they would find their own.

Our call today is also to transformation. We are to invest ourselves in every area of our community's life and have a tangible influence there. I ask our people at New Song, "Are we living out our Christian faith in this community in such a way that if we packed up and left tomorrow we'd be missed?"

I also often preach on the New Testament passage of Luke 4:14-21, particularly verses 18-19, where Jesus quotes from Isaiah 61 (and also probably Isaiah 58). This passage describes who Jesus is, what he came to do and how he came to do it. Consequently, the passage informs us (the church) on who we are, what we're here to do and where we get the power to do it. At the end of the passage Jesus powerfully points to himself as the One who inaugurates the "year of the Lord's favor"—the Jubilee year. He's the One the Old Testament prophets had long been pointing to as the Messiah of God's people. He came to preach good news to the poor, to proclaim freedom for the prisoners and recovery of sight to the blind, and to release the oppressed. The rest of his public ministry in Luke's Gospel shows him carrying out these functions.

The way Jesus ultimately brought about the year of the Lord's favor was by taking the Lord's disfavor on himself for us on the cross. It's interesting to note that in the Old Testament, the Year of Jubilee began on the Day of Atonement. In the same way, Christ's life, death and resurrection make a way for our own "Jubilee." We find our power not in our ingenuity, experience, accolades or intelligence. Our power to do the work of Christ is rooted in the very work of Christ.

How do we live this out in the community God has called us to? As the church, we are the body of Christ, the people Christ has brought into being by his power, mercy, and grace. As Jesus' ministry is comprehensive, including both proclamation and tangible deeds of mercy and justice, so likewise the church should be engaged in ministries of both word and deed.

We've tried to do this in part by living with a "parish mindset." We view our whole Sandtown community as the context of our church's ministry. There are many people in our community I have come to know who consider me their pastor; in fact, of the approximately seventy funeral services I've conducted over the past thirteen years, fewer than ten were for members of our church. The others were for people who were in some way connected to our church and who knew of New Song's reputation of "being there for the community." While I have not performed funerals with the intention of people attending our church as a result, this has happened.

I didn't anticipate such a ministry when I was in seminary, but it's been life-changing for me to share in the lives of people in their most vulnerable moments. Entering into the pain of others reminds me in a tangible way of how Christ has entered and continues to enter into my own pain. The parish mindset leads us to have a tangible presence in the community. This entails attending school functions, visiting other ministries, serving on ministry boards, having an open door where people can drop by our home, and visiting others' homes. Because of the other community development programs that operate at New Song, I've had ample opportunity to develop relationships with my neighbors.

I do not hold that every member of our community or ministry staff is automatically a member of our church, which distinguishes our "parish mindset" from a more traditional "parish model." Being a member of the church comes through faith in Jesus Christ, not by where one lives or who one works for. In fact, many of our community members already have other church homes. To say that everyone in our community is really a member of our church when many of them have been called by God to serve in other local bodies of Christ smacks of paternalism. For me, having a parish mindset means that I and our church make ourselves available to serve anyone and everyone, regardless of where (or if) they attend church.

Living out the church-based component requires adapting to specific circumstances. It's imperative that church leaders understand and respect the various cultural dynamics in force in your context. At New Song, we understand that we often need to walk in a "gracious tension." We follow the principles of Christian community development, but we are also a member of a particular church denomination (the Presbyterian Church in America). And we also take into account that we reside in a community heavily influenced by the traditional African American church. These realities sometimes are in tension with each other as we live out what it means to be the church. Doing so takes a lot of prayer, spiritual maturity and hard work.

We must also consider what I call "cultural gravity." We all live and minister out of our own unique cultural context, factoring in race, culture, gender, where we grew up, how and where we've been educated, and theological perspective. All of these impact how we do ministry. I, for example, am an African American male who grew up in the suburbs; my approach to ministry is informed by that background, even though where I minister is a different context. If we are ministering in a cultural context different from our own, we need to work harder and more intentionally to be able to speak the language of our community in a way that will be received as we intend it to be. When I prepare a sermon, I know instinctively how it communicates to people who are from where I am from. I take the extra step, however, to consider primarily how the passage communicates particularly to my neighbors from Sandtown.

The church-based component of Christian community development is best lived out in concert with the other key components. Being church-based is best expressed through *reconciliation, relocation* and *redistribution.* The ministry of the church will be *wholistic* and shaped by *listening to the community. Leadership development* of our neighbors in the community will be a consistent priority in every area of ministry, and intentionality will be given to *empowering leaders* for ministry.

Finally, church-based means that the Word of God is the final authority on matters of faith and practice in all we do. The Bible takes priority over everything—our experience, the wisdom and advice of community development experts, and what seems most pragmatic for accomplishing what we deem important. In Martin Luther King's "Letter from Birmingham Jail," he discusses how the church in Acts did not function simply like a thermometer, merely reflecting the values of the society around it. The early church's ministry functioned like a thermostat, setting the temperature in its worship, work and redeeming presence in the community around it. At the end of the day, we hope that by seeing the church as the basis for all Christian community development, our church will be a thermostat—not isolated from our community, not assimilating to it, but transforming it.

Creating a Culture of Health

By Bruce Miller

I love entering our health center. Our greeters are out front doing a great job extending the love of Jesus. It's easy to feel proud of our staff and what they accomplish every day. As the administrative leader, I admit that I particularly love when the waiting room is full. It means that people from our community are coming to see our doctors. I can be confident that bills will go out and payments will come in. It means that our business and our ministry are succeeding.

But this is not our only measure of success. Because our health center is a ministry of Lawndale Community Church (LCC), we have additional goals. LCC's mission pushes us to not be satisfied with visits as the only measure of success. LCC's mission is "to redeem the Lawndale Community, to bring Christian wholistic revitalization to the lives and environment of its residents." I can hear John Perkins saying, "We have to provide more than service if we're going to make a difference." The ingredients of a healthy community are more complicated than providing exam room visits.

Over the last three decades, we have done a great deal to create access to quality, affordable health care in North Lawndale. A number of health indicators such as the infant mortality rate and immunization rates have certainly improved. But when I think about the factors that cause our community to be less healthy than others, the biggest problems seem tough to address in an exam room.

For example, about 41 percent of adult males in our community smoke, comparing very unfavorably to the national average of about 24 percent.

Another health statistic that will challenge the future is related to weight control. According to the Sinai Community Institute, about 41 percent of adults in North Lawndale are obese, again comparing unfavorably to national statistics from the Centers for Disease Control and Prevention. From the same study we learned that 53 percent of the kids in our community were obese, comparing quite unfavorably to the CDC's national averages of less than 16 percent.

We need to work at creating a culture of health in the low-income communities we serve. Culture is what exudes from the people in the community. It is connected to the community's energy, not to the energy we offer as service providers.

How can we stimulate a culture of health? I don't know all the answers, but I can describe a few things we're doing that seem to be headed in the right direction, efforts that create energy not just for our community but also for our staff.

In 1984 our church renovated an old Cadillac dealership into a meeting room, a six-room exam clinic and a gymnasium. Over the years we filled up the meeting room with exam rooms; by 2000 it was a full-fledged health center with thirty-eight exam rooms, along with the gymnasium.

The gym was a place for basketball; it had little direct connection to the health center, but that began to change in 2001 when we joined the Diabetes Collaborative sponsored by the federal Bureau of Primary Health Care. We organized a motivated team and gave them the assignment of championing changes in how we provided chronic care.

The team organized our first disease-oriented registry and began keeping score on our performance. They hired lay diabetes educators and began talking about issues such as depression and its impact on patients with chronic illnesses. I came to their meetings and learned odd abbreviations like the HbA1c—a form of hemoglobin measured to identify a person's average plasma glucose concentration over time. (It took me months to verbally put those letters and numbers in the right order, but I got the picture.)

A theme that caught my attention was the relationship of diabetes to obesity. So when someone volunteered the idea that we use our gym to start an aerobics program, it was pretty easy to think, *Why hadn't we thought of that before?* The idea of being in the fitness business began to percolate.

We had some good fortune raising money, so we added a 9,000-square-foot addition to our building, dedicating about 3,000 square feet to fitness. The space includes what you might expect: treadmills, elliptical machines and weight-training equipment. We didn't have a lot of ready-made expertise, but the Lord led the right people to us. Over the years I've learned that the success of our programs depends heavily on who the Lord brings to us.

We opened Lawndale Christian Fitness Center in February 2005. In our first full year of operation we registered nearly 29,000 visits. Four years later, the number had gone to more than 55,000 visits per year. We offer classes with names like cardiopunch, salsaholics, Silversneakers (funded by two managed care companies) and Dr. Aerobics, led by one of our pediatricians.

Our success has easily exceeded my imagination. And what I love most about it is knowing that while we provide the resources, our patients/members are the ones who do the work of improving their health.

When I think of our fitness center, I think of my neighbor Mr. Pearson, a man in his seventies. When he learned we were building a fitness center, he asked me several times to let him know when it opened. I'd smile kindly and say, "Sure," never once thinking he would use it. Boy, did I get an earful when he learned that the center had been open for three weeks and I hadn't informed him. He quickly became our most frequent user, teaching me not to underestimate anyone. And now he is a regular at our Sunday worship services.

Then there is the Pegues family, a family of four that lives just a few blocks from LCHC. At the invitation of friends, the mother of the family joined one of our Saturday morning aerobics classes. From there she got her whole family involved. As a family they have now lost over a hundred pounds. Today Anthony, the father, is now a board member at the fitness center. We're stimulating a culture of health, and it's exciting to watch.

Since opening our fitness center in 2005 we have run a program around Christmas time called the Corporate Challenge. During one year of this fitness challenge, more than fifty staff members competed, many of whom have lost a significant amount of weight. I was among them; I shed fifteen pounds. The culture of health penetrates our staff and influences the circle of people around us.

In their introductory materials to the Wellness program they created, our staff wrote the following:

> *Wellness can be described as an expanded idea of health that reaches beyond illnesses, disabilities, or even weight loss. According to Fahey, Insel, & Roth, authors of "Fit & Well," wellness gives us "the ability to live life fully—with vitality and meaning." Simply stated, wellness brings out the best in us. It brings out the best in our relationship with our spouse and children, increases job performance, and most importantly helps us to be better men and women of God fulfilling what we are called to do.*

In terms of the CCDA's values, it's unlikely any of this would be happening if the health center were not church-based—guided by principles and goals that go well beyond simply healing people physically. I also see a connection with relocation, as relocation facilitates desiring for our neighbor and neighbor's family what we desire for ourselves. The fitness initiative was so exciting to me partly because I knew it would benefit my family. In 2012 we tripled the size of our fitness center. Now over one thousand people a day are becoming healthier through exercise.

At LCHC we strive not to be a sick-care center but a health-care center. Our goals go beyond providing care for the body. The goal of loving and creating a culture of health in our community is directly related to our being rooted in the ministry of a local church.

10

A WHOLISTIC APPROACH

Some segments of the evangelical church have placed evangelism on a pedestal higher than other scriptural admonitions governing those who follow Christ. That's understandable; historically, evangelical Christian faith emerged in part as a response to the so-called social gospel, which, to put it most simply, reduced the gospel message to feeding the hungry, serving the poor and advocating for justice. There was little if any room on the social gospel agenda for leading people to a relationship with Jesus Christ.

One can, however, make the case that an exclusive emphasis on evangelism is an overreaction to the shortcomings of the social gospel. For some segments of the evangelical movement, it seems that leading people to Christ has become the only thing that matters. Far from being legitimate ends in themselves, efforts to feed the hungry, visit the prisoner or bring comfort and aid to the poor are understood merely as means to achieve the only truly important goal: getting people saved.

Following through with this understanding, once people make a decision to follow Christ, it makes sense for the evangelist to leave the scene. It doesn't matter if new believers are still hurting, still poor, still hungry, still unemployed, still homeless, still confined to substandard housing, still being victimized by injustice—in a word, still in need of love.

When he lived on earth Jesus was a spiritual being, but he was not just a spiritual being. Luke 2:52 records that he grew in wisdom (intellectually), in stature (physically) and in favor with God (spiritually) and other people (socially). Here and in many other places, Scripture is not confined to spiritual concerns, important as they are. If we are to be imitators of Christ, then we too must grow wholistically—and help others to do the same. As Mark Sheerin writes in *Christianity Today*,

> Jesus came to earth not just to patch up a relationship between mankind and an offended Father, but to radically reconcile all things to himself. He came to bring redemption to institutions and individuals, to the realms of justice and law, to education and child-rearing, to farms, to cities, to finance—to everything. Jesus came to undo the shattered world in which man stands alone and isolated.[7]

Loving Others Wholistically

Jesus was once asked which commandment in the Law was the greatest. He responded, "Love the Lord your God with all your heart and with all your soul and with all your mind." But he quickly added, "And the second is like it: 'Love your neighbor as yourself.' All the Law and the Prophets hang on these two commandments" (Matthew 22:36-40). Clearly Jesus linked loving God with loving neighbor, implying that it's not possible to love God in the way we should unless we love our neighbor.

Think for a moment about how we love ourselves and those with whom we are closest. We don't just love our children *spiritually;* we love them *wholistically.* What if we say we love our children but ignore them when they are hungry? Is our love genuine or complete? Absolutely not.

We don't want our children to be hungry or in pain. And we want them to have access to good education so they can fulfill their potential in life. We want these things for ourselves as well, because we love ourselves. The Bible is clear that we should love our neighbors the same way.

When I (Wayne) began teaching and coaching at a public high school, a guy on the football team came to my Bible study and eventually accepted Christ. Before long I became a little frustrated with him: even with his newfound faith, his grades didn't improve. He was failing in school. After doing some investigating, however, I concluded that he was doing the best he could. He was going to class and doing his homework. He had a learning disability. The trouble he had reading didn't change when he came to Christ. He needed someone to love him like a neighbor by helping him with his reading disability.

Two boys in another family also came to Christ. But their landlord was not paying the gas bills, so their heat got turned off in the dead of winter. Accepting Christ in their hearts did not make their bodies any warmer. They needed someone to love them like a neighbor, which in this case meant organizing tenants to withhold some of their rent money to pay the gas bill directly.

The Bible does not tell us just to get people saved; it tells us we are to make disciples. If we are to make disciples, we can't quit caring about people once they accept Christ. They still need those who follow Christ to love them wholistically.

Not "Either-Or" but "Both-And"

Although we've highlighted the importance of issues such as injustice, poverty and education, we urge Christian ministries not to subordinate evangelism and discipleship. Coming to

Christ may not automatically put food on a poor family's table, but neither will providing a family with nutritious meals address their spiritual and emotional needs. A dynamic relationship with God through Christ does not solve all problems, but it does provide people with hope, with a completely new perspective and with the motivation to push forward.

Scripture does not require us to choose between inviting people into a personal relationship with Christ and meeting their material, social and emotional needs. It's not an either-or proposition; it's a both-and opportunity. In fact, to send the message that we will help people only if they come to Christ might be perceived by them as a kind of spiritual blackmail.

The irony, we believe, is that showing people that we love them wholistically and unconditionally is the most effective way to lead them to Christ. We allow people to see Christ in us when we love them with no strings attached. People who feel genuine, unconditional love are more likely to want to discover the source of this love.

Addressing Problems Wholistically

CCDA's emphasis on a wholistic approach goes beyond loving people. It includes taking a wholistic (comprehensive or multifaceted) approach to solving a community's problems. There are no simple solutions because the problems are so complex and interrelated: the breakdown of the family, crime, drug addiction, unjust social structures, substandard education, lack of morality, counterproductive government programs. People disagree on which if any of the above ought to be number one on the list of most important problems to solve.

We need church-based ministries to address all of these challenges and more wholistically, recognizing the relationships between and among them. For one thing, focusing only on one problem without considering others runs the risk of producing unintended consequences. The Hope House at Lawndale, for example, is for men who are coming out of jail or overcoming addiction. Our "Alternatives to Violence" training is open to church members and community members alike.

Both the mission statement and the vision statement of Lawndale Community Church reflect a commitment to wholistic ministry:

> LCC's mission is to redeem the "Lawndale Community." We seek to bring Christian wholistic revitalization to the lives and environment of its residents through economic empowerment, housing improvement, educational enrichment, quality affordable health care, and Christian discipleship.
>
> LCC envisions a future when Christian values undergird the attitudes and actions of Lawndale residents; when existing community people are empowered to live in harmony and security; when vacant lots and abandoned buildings are converted into new, affordable homes and rehabbed apartments; when the majority of homes are owner occupied; when high school and college graduation are accepted expectations; when job skills and employment opportunities abound; when all people have quality affordable health care; and where JESUS CHRIST IS LORD!

A Place Brimming with Shalom

by Ryan Ver Wys

"Well, let's see. We have positions open in Kenya, Nicaragua and Bellflower, California." So said the recruiter at World Renew, an international relief and development organization. It was the summer of 2000. My wife, Rachel, and I had just gotten married. Inspired by the books we'd been reading, we were looking for ways to get involved in community development, and we thought a two-year internship would be good way to test the waters.

It didn't take much deliberating for us to opt for the most exotic of the three options. A month later we left our lives in West Michigan for Southern California. Rachel worked with Open Arms Community Services, a ministry initiated by seven local congregations. While she met with neighbors and explored possibilities for ministry collaborations, I started an Individual Development Account program in south central Los Angeles with Job Starts.

We joined a beautiful, small, multiethnic congregation that met in the city of Long Beach. It drew people from all walks of life and reflected the neighborhood in which it met. We loved it. Before long, I became the youth and worship leader. After fulfilling our commitments, we decided to stay. Rachel went back to school, and I went to work full-time at the church. Between youth group and small group meetings, Sunday services, and various other activities, church demanded a lot of my time and energy. We had become Southern Californians. Our lives were busy going from one commitment to the next. Something, however, was not right.

Bob Lupton writes in *Return Flight* about neighbors who are good Christians but "un-neighbors":

> people who live on our street but contribute nothing to the well-being of our street. With the church as the center around which their busy lives revolve, they become isolated from their neighborhood.[8]

When we read this in 2003, we recognized ourselves as un-neighbors, and we didn't like it. We wanted God to help us see our neighborhood with his eyes and to use us to expand his kingdom.

For starters, we did a lot of walking, listening to our neighbors and networking with other Christians. We wanted to see what God was up to in our city. Where was he working? What was it about the current state of our city that was breaking his heart? We quickly saw that our small suburban city faced many of the same challenges of our neighboring, more stereotypically "urban" municipalities.

Reggie McNeil suggests that "the condition of our communities is the scorecard on how well the church is doing at being the people of God."[9] If this is true, it was clear our church had much work to do.

For decades, the church in our city had been a potent and positive force. In the 1960s Bellflower had by some counts the highest number of churches per capita in the United States, earning it the tagline "51 churches and no jail." But over time, while our neighbors faced a variety of symptoms stemming from relational poverty, congregations seemed content to compete with one another as purveyors of spiritual goods and services. The government and social sector had supplanted the church from its rightful role in combating poverty and the systemic brokenness that perpetuated it.

We began praying with Christians from several Bellflower congregations, imagining together what could happen if the people of God in our city began to work in coordinated unity to bless Bellflower and our shared neighbors. What if, as Eric Swanson and Sam Williams put it, "the whole church took the whole gospel to our whole city"?[10]

Birth of a Vision

We believed that if the church was more united in our obedience to Jesus' Great Commission and Commandment, Bellflower could become "a city on a hill," a place brimming with *shalom*. God's people would display love and justice in the riverbeds and under the overpasses, on every street and in every home and apartment complex. Marketplace leaders would use their business skills to advance God's mission. Artists would freely beautify blighted corners, and gifted backyard farmers could transform empty lots into community gardens. Schools would provide quality education to all of our neighbors. New support systems, informed by a biblical understanding of relational poverty, would provide dignifying help to our most vulnerable neighbors and transform the way governmental safety nets provide aid.

This lofty dream would require a movement. Shalom like this could not be achieved by any one congregation trying to do it alone. As we networked with others who loved Jesus, we discovered that the Holy Spirit had been at work drawing other servants—other churches—to the work of wholistic community development. In recent years co-conspirators have emerged to join the cause, mobilizing and applying the gifts and human resources of the body to the brokenness that surrounds us.

In 2004 we organized the nonprofit Kingdom Causes Bellflower (KCB), through which God's people are courageously taking a wholistic approach to developing community together. We know we will never experience the fullness of God's *shalom* until Christ's return, and by no means do we claim any credit or level of expertise. Yet are excited to see glimpses of God's kingdom breaking through, and we attribute this to the power of God working through his united body, the church.

Ending Homelessness

As the church's collective understanding of the complex nature of homelessness has grown, our approach has evolved. In 2005, Christians from local congregations decided instead of driving twenty miles to volunteer in soup kitchens on Skid Row they would creatively connect with the one hundred homeless neighbors within a five-mile radius of our own homes. We began a weekly outreach of breakfast and showers, preaching the gospel and praying for our hurting neighbors. We also began working at a systems level regionally in Los Angeles County, addressing the need for affordable housing.

We are honored to be a part of the Home for Good and 100,000 Homes campaigns seeking to end homelessness in our neighborhoods. These campaigns ensure that government and philanthropic funding is effectively and efficiently dispersed in a way that respects and preserves relational connectedness for those the resources are intended to help. The results are exciting. In Bellflower, in two years we witnessed a 28 percent decrease in chronic homelessness. Neighbors such as a crossing guard in our community, a veteran who'd been homeless for years, now has his own apartment. He's joined the congregation whose building stands on corner where he works each day protecting children.

Changing Schools

Several churches and nonprofits have worked for years through after-school tutoring programs to support students in the Bellflower Unified School District. As we began looking more closely at our local schools, we saw a disparity. Those in the southern part of our district—in Lakewood, a more economically prosperous area—generally had higher academic achievement and more educational options. Seeking alternative educational options for families and the infusion of healthy competition in a system stagnated by monopoly, Rachel and several other Christians passionate about education came together in an effort to create a charter school that would have smaller class sizes and emphasize classical education. While the district school board ultimately stymied the charter school in 2010, two years later it created a new, alternative school on the north side that is implementing some of the very changes advocated by the charter school group. In addition, KCB has initiated a partnership with the city volunteer center and school staff that places volunteers in one of the lowest academically performing elementary schools. Increasing educational options and God's people serving have resulted in a stronger educational system for children in our community.

Decreasing Poverty Through Employment

As we became friends with people transitioning out of homelessness or back into mainstream society from rehabilitative programs, we saw another opportunity for the church to serve our neighbors together. Local Christian business leaders and other volunteers created Good Soil Industries, a lawn maintenance social enterprise that provides second chance employment and supportive discipleship during a critical time for people with employment barriers. In addition to getting résumé building and job skills training, people with little or no previous work experience get their hands dirty and discover the dignity found in a hard day's work. They eventually transition into full-time employment elsewhere. More than a hundred churches, businesses and homeowners have made their lawn maintenance budgets missional by hiring Good Soil.

Improving Quality of Life

When the Great Recession of 2009 hit, our city had to make difficult decisions, including cutting fun community events. Recognizing that celebrative gatherings and safe community events have a direct impact on our neighborhoods, in 2009 several churches came together to fill the gap, organizing hundreds of volunteers to keep many of these events going, hosting community art festivals with international exhibitors, running holiday events at the park and ensuring that the annual Mayor's Prayer Breakfast continued. The church is wholistically blessing our community through cooperation with the city.

Bellflower's years of poorly planned housing development resulted in neighborhoods with high-density rental housing and numerous trailer parks. These neighborhoods, with their relatively affordable yet often blighted housing, became home to new immigrants and low-income working families. A small percentage of neighbors who are involved with gangs or drug trafficking have given these neighborhoods a bad reputation. KCB works to support the Christian leaders who reside in these neighborhoods, as well as to train and equip new neighbors to move to these areas. These neighbor-leaders host and run arts and sports programming for kids, as well as homework clubs, social enterprises and weekly Bible studies for youth.

It's hard to imagine being as successful as we've been without the spiritual grounding of the church and without individual congregations working together instead of looking out for themselves. When KCB was getting started, critics argued that the mission of "loving our neighbors together" was too broad and that we would have been better off picking one program and doing it well. But I feel that heeding God's call to share the gospel with the whole city requires a wide-ranging, wholistic approach, which in turn requires perseverance and the freedom to adapt. It's a call that requires servant leadership and people who seek first God's kingdom, even if it means setting our various individual congregational agendas aside.

Getting to Know Cookie

By Bethany Dudley

About twice a month in the spring and summer, people from a nearby church knock on doors in my neighborhood. They come in groups of two or three, armed with pamphlets and Bibles, with one goal: to save my soul.

I confess that I don't like people coming around to evangelize my neighborhood. I don't answer the door when I know it's them knocking.

One summer two people from this church cornered me as I was mowing my front lawn. (My suburban friends make fun of me for calling my postage-stamp plot of grass a lawn.) They wanted to discuss what would happen to my soul when I die or when the Lord returns. This particular day was especially hot. I had on a grubby pair of shorts and a T-shirt, and I was sweating profusely. I was frustrated that I had to turn the mower off to talk with them; I just wanted to finish the lawn and get a cold glass of water.

When they began talking about the end times, I looked them straight in the eye and asked if they knew Cookie. Anyone who spends any time at all on my block knows Cookie, an older woman who walks the community talking with everyone. They said no. I asked if they knew about what had happened down the block earlier that week. They said no.

I live in Chicago's West side in the neighborhood of Austin. Many consider my neighborhood to be one that you should drive through as fast as you can, but those who think that are missing out on an amazing secret. Austin is full of talented leaders, artists, entrepreneurs, mothers, fathers, teachers, and more. We have a wonderful park, the best soul food restaurant in the city, and accessible public transportation.

I believe those folks care about my soul. But they don't seem to care about my neighborhood. They don't seem to care about getting to know Cookie—God's image bearer. They don't know or seem to care about the shootings on my block. I find it hard to grasp how anyone following the same Jesus who healed the sick, called for justice and loved the marginalized can see souls to be won but fail to see the gifts, talents and needs of people bearing the image of God.

I smiled as politely as I could and said that right now my soul was more concerned about loving my neighbors and building God's kingdom than about the end times.

They went to the next house, leaving me some pamphlets with an extremely white Jesus on the front and fire on the back.

When I was eight years old I told my parents I was going to be a missionary in the city. I knew that a missionary's job was to tell people about Jesus. I loved telling people about Jesus, and I loved the city, so a missionary in the city sounded like the perfect job.

In seventh grade I was introduced to a nonprofit organization called Kids Clubs. I volunteered to help lead crafts and tell Bible stories in what was considered a "rough area." I fell in love with the children in this neighborhood, and over the next six years I worked with two other Kids Clubs. I also participated in tutoring programs, led discipleship groups and ran summer day-camps, giving me the opportunity to get to know hundreds of children and families throughout my city. I spent countless hours each week pouring my life into young people and their families. I loved it. I was doing what God had called me to do.

Yet my heart was breaking with a sense of hopelessness. Too many of the children I was preaching the gospel to were ending up in gangs, in jail, jobless and struggling with addictions. It turns out Kids Clubs taught Bible stories in creative ways, played fun games and ate great snacks, but we did not transform too many lives.

In college I had the opportunity to work for and eventually to lead an after-school program for a junior high school in Chicago. I loved the amazing teenagers I spent time with every day, yet I still felt this sense of hopelessness. The same thing was happening. Kids were getting lost in the deserts of poverty, violence, injustice and broken systems. I felt like I was trying to plug up holes in a cracking dam with duct tape. I had grown up praying, "Thy kingdom come, Thy will be done on earth as it is in heaven." But the ministry we'd been doing was more like, "Thy kingdom come in heaven so we don't have to worry about what happens on earth."

I encountered Christian community development as a college student in 1999 at a CCDA national conference. It felt like I was coming home. The people spoke the language of my heart. They put into words the thoughts and feelings I did not know how to express. Suddenly, ministry was not limited to Bible stories or getting people saved and out of the neighborhood. The conversation was no longer only about individual persons, but about entire communities and systems.

The wholistic approach promoted by the CCDA gave me hope for plugging the dam. I discovered ministry that engages not just the spiritual but also the social, economic, political, cultural, emotional, physical, moral, judicial and educational dimensions of individuals and communities in order to bring about kingdom transformation.

There is much brokenness in Austin. It does not yet fully reflect the kingdom of God. But the hopelessness I often felt before encountering the CCDA approach to ministry has disappeared. I have witnessed the power that lies behind relocation, reconciliation, redistribution, leadership development, empowerment and listening to the community. All these values and commitments tie into church-based, wholistic ministry.

I'm encouraged by the transformation that has taken place in communities such as Lawndale in Chicago and Sandtown in Baltimore. But what really gives me hope are the small success stories I witness in my own community. Stories about people such as Cookie, who walks back and forth from her house to the liquor store a few times a day and often stops by my house to talk.

Cookie and I have talked about her life experiences and her thoughts about the neighborhood. I once asked her what she was really good at, and she laughed off the question. Unfazed, I told her I thought she was great with the neighborhood kids. And I meant it; I'd observed that most of the time she had at least one neighborhood child in tow, and each one listened to what she had to say.

One night at about 11:00 I heard a pounding on my door. I opened it to find Cookie standing there with a huge smile on her face. She'd come by my house twice earlier that day but I wasn't home, and she knew I'd want to hear what she had to say. A local elementary school teacher had asked Cookie to be an official volunteer in her classroom.

A student in this teacher's classroom had a discipline problem. The teacher had seen Cookie with him on multiple occasions and could tell that the boy listened to her and respected her. Cookie could not wait to tell me her news.

I cannot tell you today that Cookie has been saved, has gotten a great job and no longer has a drinking problem. But I *can* tell you that she has felt valued, listened to, loved. She has been able to use the gifts God has given her and to experience, whether she knows it or not, a taste of the kingdom.

There are no easy answers to the brokenness found in under-resourced communities. Some will say it is a spiritual problem; others say it's political; still others blame systemic injustice. My experience has led me to conclude that it's all these things and more, and that throughout Scripture the Lord constantly reminds his people that he cares not only for the spiritual well-being of people but for their physical and emotional well-being too.

Wholeness occurs when nothing is missing or broken. That's what the kingdom looks like, the kingdom we're to pray for on earth as it is in heaven. My desire is to live in such a way that my neighbors cannot help but ask me why I live this way. When they do, I respond, "Let me tell you about Jesus."

11

EMPOWERMENT

Each of the CCDA's eight core principles interacts with at least one or two if not several of the others. This is certainly the case with empowerment. In the chapter on redistribution, for example, we discussed empowerment in the context of economic development, that is, empowering people by helping them gain greater control of their economic or material resources. The process of developing leaders similarly includes empowering others by giving them the authority to make decisions and being willing to accept those decisions even when we disagree. We will discuss this leadership development aspect of empowerment in more detail later in this chapter.

If the word *empower* is used casually, it can come across as patronizing. It helps to recognize that empowering in the context of Christian community development is ultimately about releasing the power of the Holy Spirit in the lives of individuals and in their neighborhoods and communities. The CCDA's emphasis on empowering is not about giving some people power or influence over others. Instead, it recognizes that the Holy Spirit is our "empowerer," the one who gives us the power to live out the gospel.

Thus, empowering others takes place within a context of caring, a context of love. The words of Martin Luther King Jr. come to mind:

> Power without love is reckless and abusive, and love without power is sentimental and anemic. Power at its best is love implementing the demands of justice, and justice at its best is power correcting everything that stands against love.[11]

Empowering others will likely entail increasing the economic resources of underprivileged individuals and communities. But material resources are not the immediate or even the ultimate focus of empowerment. Consider Peter in Acts 3. As he and John are on their way to the temple, a man who was crippled from birth gets their attention and asks for money. Says Peter, "Silver or gold I do not have, but what I do have I give you. In the name of Jesus Christ of Nazareth, walk." Peter shared not wealth but the power of God.

Economic Empowerment

We see in the Bible two principles or admonitions that, at least at first glance, appear to be in tension with each other. On the one hand, caring for the poor, the weak and vulnerable, the disenfranchised, the outcast, or those who are grieving or struggling in some way is clearly is a high-priority agenda item for followers of Christ. But on the other hand, the Bible consistently requires those in need to participate in their recovery to the extent they are able.

Within this context, then, empowering people with respect to material resources constitutes an important aspect of Christian community development.

In the Old Testament, particularly in Deuteronomy 24 and

Leviticus 19, God instituted the gleaning system as a way to care for the poor and vulnerable. The farmers who owned the land and did the work harvested their crops, so they got the first and best fruits as a reward for their labor. But in accordance with the gleaning system, farmers were allowed to go through their fields only one time. Anything that was left behind or dropped on the ground was available for any widow, alien, orphan or poor person to come and harvest. This was God's way of empowering the powerless.

Two important principles can be drawn from this Old Testament system. First, there must be opportunity for all people to get their needs met. As human beings we have the moral responsibility to look out for others. Life is not all about acquiring and keeping everything we can, even if we think we deserve it. God wants us to share. Second, however, the person who has the need must be willing to work for what they get. The widow, alien, orphan or poor person had to go into the farmer's field and pick up the crops they needed or wanted. They had to work. Otherwise, they would go without.

This point is made rather starkly by Paul in 2 Thessalonians 3:10: "For even when we were with you, we gave you this rule: 'The one who is unwilling to work shall not eat.'" This same principle is echoed in Jesus' parable of the talents, as recorded in Matthew 25:14-30. Someone who is in authority goes on a trip and leaves behind talents (units of money) to three of his servants. One of them gets five talents, one gets two, and the third gets one. The first two servants put their talents to work and double what had been entrusted to them. The third, however, buries his talent in the ground. He does nothing. When the boss returns, it is the third servant, even though he'd been given the least to work with, who gets punished, presumably for being irresponsible, if not downright lazy.

Affirming People's Dignity

All human beings, because they were created in the image of God, possess inherent dignity. When the two principles cited above are in operation, this dignity is affirmed. The first principle makes it possible for people to take care of themselves and their vulnerable loved ones without having to beg or steal. The second principle allows people to achieve some measure of self-respect because to some extent they earned what they are receiving, which empowers them with dignity.

When people participate—as opposed to having everything simply given to them—their dignity is affirmed. The late Millard Fuller, founder of Habitat for Humanity, liked to tell the story of a housing project in Atlanta that former President Jimmy Carter took part in. A few months after the project was complete, Millard found himself in the area and decided to drive through the neighborhood. He saw a young boy playing in the yard of the very house the former President had helped build. He called the boy over and asked him how he liked his new house.

"I love it," the boy replied.

Millard followed up, "You know who worked on your house, don't you?"

The boy replied, "Yes. My dad!"

This boy's father, because he'd participated in his own empowering, gained dignity not just in his own eyes but, perhaps more importantly, in the eyes of his young son.

Many charity programs, though well intended, strip people of their dignity by doing for them instead of empowering them to do for themselves. The result is that dependency is created or amplified instead of being addressed and solved. As has been well documented and analyzed, creating dependency (and the sense of entitlement that goes with it) was an unintended consequence of some of the landmark welfare programs of the 1960s. Bob Lupton's book *Toxic Charity* explores the negative effects some forms of modern charity have on the very people meant to benefit from it. (It also provides models for charitable groups who want to help—not sabotage—those they desire to serve.)

Avoiding Dependency

The CCDA maintains that empowerment functions as the antidote to dependency. The goal is to make sure that the people we are helping are at some point in the future able to help themselves. As with many things, this can be far more easily said than done. But a good place to start is to ask the following of the person in need of help:

- What will it take for you not to need anything from us in one year's time?

- What has to happen over the next year for you to get to a place where you can help others instead of needing help?

The next step is to work with the person to make sure his or her answers are both sincere and realistic. Perhaps someone wants to own his own house. To do that he needs a job. To get a job he might need a new suit or some leads for where to seek employment. The ministry can do its part by helping him purchase appropriate clothing and perhaps providing guidance in his job search. But his end of the deal must include working hard to find a job and being committed to holding the job once he has it, even if it's not perfect or ideal. (Not many jobs are.)

It's important to maintain the commitment not to do for people what they are able to do for themselves. There is a difference between coming alongside and supporting others, and doing what they, for their own good, can and should be doing for themselves. This includes helping people to come up with their own game plan for getting from where they are to where they want to be. This approach is ultimately what empowers them.

This can be difficult work. It's hard to be in a position of having to judge, for example, whether someone is just trying to avoid taking responsibility or whether he or she is struggling with deep-seated emotional issues that can be hard to identify, let alone to address. In these instances, there is clearly a role for professional counselors to help people deal with whatever is keeping them from helping themselves. This too is a form of empowerment.

Empowering Leaders

Given our conviction that developing indigenous leaders is central to community development, it's important to provide some perspective on empowering leaders. We are convinced that, while some people possess innate leadership abilities, leadership is something that can be learned, taught and "caught" through effective modeling. We've seen many examples of people who on paper didn't fit the leadership mold but who nevertheless became effective leaders as they acquired skills and gained confidence.

However, if people are to become effective leaders, they need first of all to be given opportunities. This includes opportunities to fail so they can learn from their mistakes. Those who are trying to develop other leaders sometimes must fight the temptation to do everything themselves just because they can do it better. With this approach, others will never learn. Instead, give people responsibilities commensurate with their skills and then resist the temptation to micromanage. It's a joyful experience for everyone when people do what they once thought they would never be able to do.

The goal of a leader is similar to the goal of parent, to do such a good job developing and empowering others that we are no longer needed. The best Christian leaders are those who think not about what is best for themselves or their careers, but what is best over the long haul for the kingdom of God.

Finally, empowering others requires that we distinguish between giving others authority and giving them resources, including practical knowledge. They need both. If we give people authority without giving them resources, we may be unwittingly setting them up to fail. Knowing how to access a ministry's bank account, having the keys to all the rooms in the buildings, knowing whom to call with a plumbing problem—all these things and more might seem like trivial matters until something goes wrong and the person who's been put in charge has not been empowered with the answers.

In sum, empowering others is rooted in an attitude of humility and generosity. It's about sharing resources and giving away power in responsible ways for the sake of God's kingdom and for the sake of the poor and voiceless, who occupy a special place in that kingdom.

Marina's Story

By Christine Brooks Nolf

As with many Christian community development ministries, Mika Community Development Corporation (MCDC) was founded with the belief that our neighbors have a vision for our community and assets that can be directed toward that vision. Early in my community development work, a mentor (Ron Bueno) advised me to pay attention to the quiet, faithful neighbors who kept showing up but did not have much to say. His experience had been that the first wave of neighbors to jump in are loud and have lots of ideas. They are quick to share their thoughts and ideas, but they tend to disengage once they begin to understand that we will all have to work together over a long period of time in order to act on their ideas or bring about lasting change. In contrast, the neighbors who had been patiently observing and at times timidly participating will eventually rise up.

That is exactly what happened with Marina. A short Mexican woman with big dark brown eyes, Marina's hair is long and black, and her smile explodes quickly, occupying her whole face. She was one of the first women I met; she quickly became my first friend in my new neighborhood. But her timid demeanor does not immediately scream "neighborhood leader."

At first, Marina was especially shy. In neighborhood meetings she rarely spoke. She often seemed uncomfortable or distressed and kept mostly to herself. Yet she always showed up for the neighborhood meetings. In fact, she was often the first to arrive and was clearly the most faithful. When we started Saturday work projects in the park, Marina brought her children and even her next-door neighbor. When we needed representatives at City Hall to advocate for lights in our alley, Marina packed her baby in the stroller and came to the council chambers to offer support. She was not our speaker, but she was there nonetheless to advocate for her community.

When the city park commissioners came to celebrate the lighting installment with our neighbors, I noticed Marina approaching them to welcome and thank them, even though her English is very limited. Timid though she was, she was willing push herself for the benefit of our community. Marina says that life began to change for her when she got involved with the Neighborhood Action Committee. Her constant look of distress in the early days was fully warranted. Her husband worked in roofing, a seasonal job. If the weather was good, he got work. If the weather was bad, the family had no income. It was a constant challenge for them to pay the rent. On top of that, Marina's husband had a drinking problem, which exacerbated the financial problems and at times led to abuse at home. Finally, Marina got tired of living in fear, and she called the police. At that point, she knew she was not alone. The stories of their struggles with finances and marriage the women shared in the Neighborhood Action Committee gave Marina the strength and courage to make a difficult decision. And it was through the network of the Neighborhood Action Committee that Marina began finding work cleaning houses so that she could provide for her family.

As MCDC's work expanded, we started a small Bible study in the neighborhood. It was there, in a neighbor's home, that Marina accepted Christ as her Savior. She was an eager learner—whether the focus of her learning was the Bible, the city or her neighbors' stories. She has not only embraced the values we decided upon as a Neighborhood Action Committee, but she has become the compass of the group, often calling us back to the original intention of serving the neighborhood and upholding our agreed-on values, not the least of which is living as examples of love in our community.

As the longest standing member of our Neighborhood Action Committee, Marina holds a place of respect in the community. She is still usually quiet in meetings, but when she does speak it is to acquaint new neighbors with our purpose and to make sure our focus is on giving of ourselves to our community as living examples of Christ's love.

Marina has lived this example as a mother, a wife and a neighbor. When her husband was released from jail, she received him back, though with stipulations that have made for a healthier home for them and their children. With both of them able to provide income, they moved to a bigger apartment of their own, no longer having to rent out their bedrooms in order to pay the rent. Marina no longer has that constant look of distress on her face. Instead, she exudes peace and joy. And she is constantly on the lookout for other neighbors who wear their distress like she used to wear it.

Although Marina is shy, she is also bold. In fact, she is empowered. She reaches out to neighbors who are struggling. She brings them to work with her. She babysits their children. She brings their names and situations to the Neighborhood Action Committee for prayer and resources. She emboldens others to call the police if they need to. She challenges people to get to know their neighbors and to be as generous as possible in sharing what little they have. People trust her because they have seen her do all the things she is asking others to do. No one can argue with the witness of her life. And many of us remember what her life looked like before.

When I think about what led Marina to lead an empowered life that has a positive impact on our community, I can pull out three key, interrelated factors.

First, Marina became part of a group of neighbors whose purpose is to intentionally build community. As people came together, they created a network of relationships and support that minimized their isolation and connected them with the world outside the neighborhood.

This community network was the catalyst of the second factor, namely, Marina getting a job. Her financial independence was key to helping her recognize her power.

Third, in the context of supportive relationships and consistent work, Marina came to see herself as a woman who had been created in the image of God and who has a purpose in the world. It's hard to imagine a greater source of empowerment than that. In recognizing her identity as a beloved child of God who had talents to offer her family and her community, Marina began not only to respect herself but to warrant respect from those around her.

Through the work of our Neighborhood Action Committee, Marina has had numerous opportunities to express her opinions and ideas and to see others, including people in positions of power, respond to her. Part of being empowered for her was coming to understand that her voice and abilities truly matter and are making a difference in individual lives and in our community as a whole.

It brings me deep joy when I see Marina's daughter pack up her baby in the stroller and head out to the Neighborhood Action Committee. Instead of a legacy of victimization and distress, Marina has given her children a legacy of service and respect. Together, they plan and work toward their vision of a safe, healthy Costa Mesa that both reflects and builds the kingdom of God.

AFTERWORD

Incarnating the Good News of the Kingdom

By Noel Castellanos

Twenty-three years ago my family packed up our home in San Jose and moved to La Villita, a barrio of more than 100,000 residents, mostly of Mexican descent, near Chicago's lower west side. As a third-generation Mexican American and son of migrant workers, I find it a wonderful place to call home. Nearly a thousand thriving businesses and taquerias line 26th Street. There are several fantastic parks. Friendly faces are almost always willing to offer a passing "Buenos dias."

But La Villita is also riddled with difficulties. We have more than our share of unemployment and crime, as well as the dubious honor of having Cook County Jail located in our barrio. Additionally, half of the immigrant population is undocumented, so poverty is an ever-present challenge.

I can't think of a better place in the United States to work out what it means to be an agent of God's kingdom.

My journey to La Villita began when my wife and I were

doing ministry with an evangelical organization in San Jose. The organization was primarily concerned with getting kids "saved," an impulse I shared. But the longer I worked there, the more I realized that the everyday, systemic struggles of our neighbors—parents who struggled to make ends meet, children who were engulfed in drugs and gang violence, public schools with a 50 percent dropout rate—required a wholistic solution that included, but wasn't limited to, evangelism.

As I grew discontent with the incomplete approach to community ministry I was participating in, I encountered the work of Dr. John Perkins. He had come to lecture at City Team Ministries in San Jose about Christian community development. As I heard him unfold his understanding of the Christian mission, a robust theology stirred my heart.

I spoke with Dr. Perkins following his lecture, and he invited me to come to a meeting in Chicago where a group of Christians were forming an entity that would be committed to a new way of living. I took him up on his offer, and in that meeting, the organization that would become the Christian Community Development Association (CCDA) was born.

During that visit to Chicago, one of the members of the host church invited me to dinner at the only Chinese restaurant in La Villita. My eyes popped open as we drove the streets of that neighborhood. I couldn't believe that such a place existed in the Midwestern United States. People often remark that La Villita feels like an escape not just from Chicago but from America. Throughout dinner, I kept thinking, *This is the kind of place I want to live.*

When I returned to San Jose, I told my wife that I had found a neighborhood we needed to pray about living in. In a matter of months, we packed up our family and moved there.

What is most fascinating about my journey to La Villita is what happened when I told my parents I was moving there.

"You're moving to La Villita?" they asked. "That's the neighborhood we used to visit when you were a kid."

Suddenly, fading memories flooded back into my mind. When my parents were living and working in Indiana and Michigan, they would travel to Chicago. I remembered visiting a largely Mexican community there. To break the monotony of working in the fields, my parents would take me to eat tacos and tortas and to see Spanish-language films at a movie theater that is now a large retail mall, filled with local vendors. Today, when I walk past that old theater, I think, *Isn't it just like God to bring me full circle like that?*

Living in La Villita hasn't always been easy. When Christians talk about the poor, there is a very strong reaction against the idea that we have to move among the people we serve. But I knew that, like Christ, I had to dwell among the people I loved and wanted to reach. We can't just do ministry *to* a people; we must do ministry *among* a people.

But when you actually do this—particularly in a complicated context like La Villita—it takes time to figure out what to do exactly.

I began by volunteering at a clinic established by our partner church and teaching art at a local school. I searched for people to disciple in their journey with Jesus, a task often easier said than done. In San Jose, I realized, many Christians had, like me, truncated the gospel. In La Villita, I had to work out what a more fully integrated expression of the good news looked like.

I've been a part of this barrio for more than two decades now, and through it all, I've developed a greater understanding of the complexity of being a faithful agent of the good news of the kingdom in an underresourced community. Instead of promoting a one-dimensional gospel that only offers hope in the world to come, I have become convinced that we can experience a taste of the kingdom here on earth—even in a place like La Villita. More than anything, I've developed a framework for those of us who are committed to being agents of the kingdom in the most vulnerable neighborhoods of our nation and world.

This framework, along with the CCDA's eight components, is the guiding principle for what we do through Christian community development. It is built on the most foundational image of the Christian faith: the cross.

Incarnation

The Word became human and made his home among us. He was full of unfailing love and faithfulness. (John 1:14 NLT)

At the center of God's salvation narrative is the amazing idea that through Christ God invades our human reality—*en carne,* or in the flesh—to rescue and restore creation. I love the way *The Message* renders this verse: "The Word became flesh and blood, and moved into the neighborhood."

A careful reading of Scripture makes it clear that the neighborhood Jesus moved into looked like the kind many in the CCDA dwell in. When people began to suspect that Jesus might be a prophet or the Messiah, the question was often raised: "Can anything good come from Nazareth or Galilee?" (e.g., John 1:46; 7:41). Jesus, it seems, was from the 'hood, the wrong side of the tracks.

We conclude that in the incarnation of Christ, God not only enters human reality but a social and political reality rooted not in the center of religious and political power but among the poor and marginalized. I am inclined to say that all effective ministry, regardless of context, must be incarnational. This is the linchpin for all effective kingdom ministry—especially in vulnerable neighborhoods.

There are four elements that must be considered as we pursue incarnational ministries:

- *Proximity.* In the incarnation God draws close to human suffering and sinfulness so we might know his love. Reflecting on Jesus' example has caused many of us in the CCDA to conclude that if we are going to have a kingdom impact in underresourced communities, we must be close to the neighbors we seek to love and befriend. This decision comes with huge challenges, but as we have seen, it is of utmost importance to the work of the CCDA, because it allows us to be present with people.

- *Relationship.* Jesus had the unique ability to make everyone feel loved and important. That became the foundation of his influence and impact on those around him. Moving from seeing our neighbors as targets of ministry to seeing them as friends and even brothers and sisters in Christ begins with establishing relationships. Once these relationships deepen, we earn the right to speak into people's lives and the credibility to share our stories in a way that touches peoples' hearts and souls. Through these relationships we are also transformed, through the love and concern of our neighbors.

- *Solidarity.* When we live in a neighborhood, the problems of the people in that community are no longer *their* problems; they become *our* problems too. This type of solidarity is one reason the ministry of Jesus was so powerful. He was not afraid to enter into the suffering and pain of those he encountered. Before Jesus died for people's sins, he listened and touched and empathized with their anguish and their pain. We must do no less.

- *Humility.* Philippians 2 reminds us that though Christ was God—with access to every divine privilege and power—he emptied himself of it in order to enter our world. When I see other Christians getting excited to move into underresourced communities, I often fear that they'll assume a self-congratulatory attitude. I'm afraid they'll charge in thinking they will fix and save everyone they meet. Instead, we need the humility of Christ as we follow him in this world.

For many, the idea of incarnating one's life into a poor neighborhood and the components that are part of it—proximity, relationship, solidarity and humility—may seem radical. But as I often remind our CCDA partners, this is nothing more than following the pattern of Jesus, the God-turned-Galilean.

Proclamation and Formation

Therefore, go and make disciples of all the nations, baptizing them in the name of the Father and the Son and the Holy Spirit. Teach these new disciples to obey all the commands I have given you. And be sure of this: I am with you always, even to the end of the age. (Matthew 28:19-20 NLT)

In many evangelical churches today the Great Commission hangs as a wall plaque or hallway painting or even on a curbside jumbotron for all to see. This is understandable: a call to take the good news of God's love to a sinful world is at the heart of the Christian faith. Unfortunately, the call to the formation of disciples—"teach them to obey"—is often demoted or ignored.

Many churches target poor neighborhoods outside their community with "shock and awe" evangelism campaigns, with little or no knowledge of what others are doing in that same community. An example might be a suburban church taking a summer mission trip into the 'hood or a developing nation. Hundreds of young people, trained in the verbal proclamation of some variation of the "four spiritual laws," practice their evangelistic messages on folks from poor neighborhoods who "need Jesus." Often pastors from churches within the neighborhood stumble upon invitations promoting these events right down the street from their church.

I call this approach "drive-by evangelism." It is neither sensitive nor effective. In fact, it has the potential to damage kingdom efforts.

Matthew 28 presents proclamation and formation as two sides of the same coin. Our Great Commission task is to make disciples and to reinforce the teachings of Jesus in the lives of his followers. This includes keeping the poor and the marginalized at the center of our ministry activity. Churches cannot accept an unbalanced focus on the verbal proclamation of the gospel while brushing the formation of Christ-followers under the ministerial rug.

Unfortunately, some in Christendom have gone to another extreme. Reacting against a "proclamation only" approach to the good news, they accomplish good works but almost ignore the "make disciples" part of these commission verses, failing to tell the story of God's love through Christ.

As we live incarnationally, we need both of these critical tasks. Ultimately, it is strong disciples, committed to living out their faith in tough places, that will bring about lasting transformation in our communities.

Demonstration of Compassion

> Pure and genuine religion in the sight of God the Father means caring for orphans and widows in their distress and refusing to let the world corrupt you. (James 1:27 NLT)

Two of the most powerful and poignant of Jesus' teachings are found in the story of the good Samaritan (Luke 10) and the end-times teaching of the sheep and the goats (Matthew 25). Both of these passages, along with James's words above, push us to recalibrate our understanding of true faith as having the poor and the vulnerable at the center of our concern for the world.

It seems every time the Gospel writers turn around, they find Jesus conversing with someone who is suffering, needy, sick, dying or enduring some kind of oppression. Our response to these individuals, Jesus reminds us, reveals whether or not we truly have experienced God's love and salvation. Compassion received, according to Jesus, breeds compassion shared with others.

Even in a wealthy "Christian" nation, there is still great need. The most devastated and neglected neighborhoods are often located in the shadows of unimaginable abundance and opulence. While the skyline of Chicago can be seen from many playgrounds in our west side neighborhood, for many of our youth, the benefits of the Magnificent Mile seem to be worlds away.

To make matters even more complicated, it seems that an overwhelming majority of the poor in the United States are people of color, making even well-intentioned efforts to bring about change in poor neighborhoods wrought with racial and cultural misunderstandings and conflicts.

Bob Lupton, a lifetime board member of the CCDA, raises an important issue in his book *Toxic Charity*: in our efforts to help the poor, especially from outside the community, we often create ministries and programs that actually hurt the people we desire to serve. Compassion without incarnation can devastate the people we seek to serve by making them into objects or targets.

Not long ago I visited a food pantry in Texas that had just completed a major renovation of their facility. It was a beautiful place to pass out food. At the end of a tour of this awesome building, the director shared that there were families in their program that they had been serving for over twenty years. I had to ask if the goal of their ministry was to keep people dependent on their support year after year. This was, needless to say, an awkward moment in the conversation.

By contrast, when compassion is rooted in incarnation, and when the goal of our ministry efforts is both individual and community empowerment, we can better discern the effects of our actions. Those of us who live in neighborhoods with extreme need have to constantly make decisions about the best way to help these individuals. Appropriate demonstration of compassion as an expression of kingdom ministry is biblical, but it does have its limits.

Restoration and Development

> Work for the peace and prosperity of the city where I sent you into exile. Pray to the LORD for it, for its welfare will determine your welfare. (Jeremiah 29:7 NLT)

Perhaps the greatest contribution the CCDA has made to the body of Christ is to elevate the kingdom ministry of restoration and development in the most underresourced neighborhoods of the United States. When we consider Jeremiah's words, we conclude that in the same way God cares for people, he cares for neighborhoods and cities—especially those in ruins.

Over fifty years ago Dr. Perkins and his wife, Vera Mae, returned to Mississippi from Southern California to establish the first Christian community development ministry among the rural poor of that state. While he felt called to the proclamation of the good news, his vision included a clear focus on racial reconciliation and community development. He saw not only the mandate to care for people's souls but also the call to care for the human needs of his new neighbors. He didn't want to just focus on charity but also to make certain people had the skills and the resources they needed to live godly and productive lives.

The concept of redistribution that John began to talk about in those early days had nothing to do with government handouts, but rather the linking of resources and opportunity to local efforts that would result in justice and empowerment, with the church leading the way. Economic and community development were central to the strategy of Christian community development from the early days; we saw the connection between adequate housing, employment, quality education and the presence of local churches, and a family's ability to thrive and flourish. Like Jeremiah, we realize that addressing the comprehensive needs of the community is a calling from God. When we commit to this kingdom ministry from within a community, instead of gentrifying neighborhoods for outsiders, we create healthy communities for current residents.

Nehemiah echoes this idea. "If it pleases the king, and if you are pleased with me," Nehemiah said, "send me to Judah to rebuild the city where my ancestors are buried" (Nehemiah 2:5 NLT). His calling is instructive for those who feel a call to the work of restoration and development. In the same way God called Jeremiah and other prophets to speak truth to the people of Israel—in the same way he called Ezra to rebuild the temple—God called Nehemiah to rebuild Jerusalem.

For many of us, the only time we have heard a message on the book of Nehemiah has been related to general leadership principles or to a church building program. But while there are great leadership lessons to learn from his life, the historical significance of Nehemiah is the rebuilding of the broken walls of Jerusalem. God called this exiled Jew with a government job in the Persian Empire to take a leave of absence and return to the city of his ancestors as an expression of kingdom ministry.

In the partnership that was established between Nehemiah

and Ezra, we see that the restoration of the temple and the development of the city were vital for the well-being of the community. The condition of the city walls and the spiritual condition of the people were intertwined. In the same way, our spiritual lives and communal lives are enmeshed today. On a planet with seven billion people, it is important to realize that the majority of people on our planet do not have the standard of living we enjoy in the United States. We must ask why we have the level of poverty and unhealthy neighborhoods that exist in the shadows of our unequaled wealth and prosperity. Could this global misalignment also be a spiritual missed opportunity?

Confrontation of Injustice

You trample the poor,
    stealing their grain through taxes and unfair rent.
Therefore, though you build beautiful stone houses,
    you will never live in them.
Though you plant lush vineyards,
    you will never drink wine from them.
For I know the vast number of your sins
    and the depth of your rebellions.
You oppress good people by taking bribes
    and deprive the poor of justice in the courts.
(Amos 5:11-12 NLT)

Most Christians have an easy time acknowledging individual human sinfulness. But when it comes to the sinfulness of institutions, systems and structures, things seem less clear. Yet the Bible teaches that we do not battle against flesh and blood but against powers and principalities of darkness (Ephesians 6:12). The more serious believers get about addressing the needs of the poor and marginalized, the more we are able to see that it is not just the bad behavior of individual people that creates poverty and despair but also the oppressive systems at play.

With increased awareness of the Bible's testimony of the God of justice, especially in the Old Testament, there have emerged in recent years numerous conferences and organizations putting justice at the forefront of their mission. They are rediscovering the part of Jesus' ministry revealed in the synagogue at Nazareth:

> The Spirit of the LORD is upon me,
>   for he has anointed me to bring Good News to the poor.
> He has sent me to proclaim that captives will be released,
>   that the blind will see,
> that the oppressed will be set free. (Luke 4:18 NLT)

The barrage of emails, books, videos and TV programs focusing on injustices—the environment, hunger, clean water, sex trafficking, genocide—can desensitize or overwhelm us. This overload is made easier when we live incarnationally because we see firsthand the systems and policies that negatively impact the children and families we love.

In the African American community, we witness the negative impact of the penal system on young black men. In the Latino community, we see that less than 50 percent of high school students are graduating, with even fewer entering and completing college. With the recent mortgage meltdown, entire neighborhoods in U.S. inner cities have been destabilized as families have been forced to abandon their homes.

Living in these communities helps us identify and address the systemic problems behind these trends. Instead of being driven or motivated by issues we learn about in the news, we begin with addressing the injustices in our own communities. Lifetime CCDA board member Mary Nelson likes to remind us that instead of only focusing our efforts on pulling people out of the river who are drowning, we need to go upstream to find out who's pushing them into the river in the first place. Digging deep to address the root causes of poverty and oppression is an essential aspect of kingdom ministry.

When It All Comes Together

When my family first moved to La Villita, we began to follow up on patients who attended the Lawndale Christian Health Center and expressed interest in pastoral care. Through our involvement in the local schools and the health center, and through relationships established with our neighbors, we were able to start a Bible study that grew into a church with a focus on Christian community development.

This enabled us to start an after-school program for local students at the urging of their parents. We created opportunities for home ownership, and we organized neighbors to stand up against gang violence. We worked hard to create a culture of empowerment for our kids, encouraging them to prepare for college. With the adults, a major aspect of our ministry was connecting people with jobs and helping them create new businesses.

The more we attempted to live out a kingdom approach to ministry in our Mexican barrio, the more I came across an issue that that was negatively impacting the residents in the community. What I found out from both parents and young people as I got to know them was that many of them lacked proper documentation. Many had come to the United States for jobs that many Americans did not want. Some came to our barrio, often risking their lives, to work hard at low-paying jobs in order to make a life for themselves and their children.

As we became aware of this issue, we attempted to help a number of our members and friends get immigration counseling. We hoped it would lead to some type of visa or legal documentation. Instead, we rushed headlong into a broken immigration system that made it almost impossible for individuals coming into our country to establish themselves as legal residents or citizens. It became apparent that to truly help my immigrant brothers and sisters I would need to work to change our broken immigration laws.

After ten years of working on this issue, as of this writing we have a very real chance of seeing comprehensive immigration reform in America. I am even more excited that evangelical Christians have stepped up to see this issue as a justice concern close to the heart of God.

I don't tell this story to congratulate myself. Any progress we've made is a result of God's good graces. Instead, I hope to show the power of incarnation. When I chose to live side by side with my Mexican American brothers and sisters in La Villita, I became aware of their situations and struggles. I began to realize that teaching them more Bible verses or giving them another bag of groceries or a warm jacket were not adequate to address the vast range of issues they were facing. We had to commit ourselves to proclamation and formation, demonstration of compassion, restoration and development, and confrontation of injustice.

Most mornings I begin my day with a run through my neighborhood. I cherish this time because I get to see my community come to life. As my feet pound the sidewalks of La Villita, I smile at children heading off to school, wave to merchants on 26th Street opening their shops and pray for my neighbors. As I round my final corner, my heart fills with love for the people who live here like it did when I first moved here.

My family and I have stayed in La Villita for twenty-three years. Through it all I've become more convinced that God wants those who follow him to become agents of the good news of the kingdom in the most vulnerable neighborhoods of our world. The old paradigms, which compartmentalize and truncate the work of the kingdom, are inadequate to accomplish this task.

When we minister in underresourced communities and only focus on proclamation and formation, it is not enough.

When we simply focus on the demonstration of compassion, it is not enough.

When our efforts only address restoration and development, it is not enough.

And, no matter how important, when we only strive for the confrontation of injustice, it is not enough.

But when we embrace a kingdom approach to ministry alongside our neighbors, our life and our message truly become good news. With Jesus as our example, may we become pioneers who heed God's call to incarnate ourselves as agents of the kingdom.

APPENDIX 1

A Snapshot of CCDA

In every struggling neighborhood of our nation there are fathers, mothers, sons and daughters who are striving to survive the hardships of life and are in need of restoration. These individuals and the communities where they live matter to God, and they matter to Christian Community Development Association. Over twenty-five years ago, CCDA came into existence to support Christ-followers from diverse backgrounds and denominations who are committed to ministering in the name of Christ in poor and marginalized communities. Today, we are as committed to this vision as we have ever been.

Dr. John Perkins has been our Moses for all of these years, and we are grateful for his inspirational leadership, which continues to guide us to this day. But this movement is no longer carried by any one individual or local ministry. All who are part of the extended familia of CCDA are integral to making this vision a reality. We are CCDA!

National Conference

For the last quarter century, men and women from across the nation have gathered every year at our CCDA national conference.

To many observers our gathering resembles a family reunion more than a typical Christian event where people assemble to gain information. At our annual fall conference, we come together to connect with other leaders who understand our unique calling to live, work and raise our families in tough places. We are inspired as we listen to other grassroots Nehemiahs and Ezras who may not be household names but are living out the principles and values of Christian community development. Finally, we come together to be trained and equipped by peers and by experts in various aspects of CCD ministry. If you have never attended one of our CCDA conferences, you have missed a glimpse of what the kingdom will look like. You have also missed my morning runs, which have become a tradition over the last decade.

CCDA Institute and Immersion

The CCDA Institute is the educational and training arm of our association. We offer workshops and training on the eight components of CCD. Three years ago, under the leadership of my good friend and coworker Dave Clark, we began to offer our ministry training during one week in Chicago. Participants in this immersion experience, which is attended by no more than ninety leaders, are literally immersed in our philosophy of ministry and are taught by a faculty of CCD experts and practitioners. Though this week-long training is not as flashy as our national conference, it transforms those who attend. Immersion alumni testify how this one week has revolutionized their ministries. These leaders are not only learning the principles of CCD but are also gaining the skills to implement them back home. If you and your leaders are looking for a training experience to help your community ministry efforts become more effective, this may be the most strategic investment you can make.

Leadership Cohort

Perhaps the most important initiative that we have started in CCDA in the last decade is our leadership cohort program. With the incredible leadership of my good friend and board member John Liotti, we created a space where leaders in our association between the ages of twenty-five and forty could come together and be infused with the DNA of Christian community development.

Within the last seven years we have seen over 125 young leaders participate in this program. Not only has it resulted in our cohort members forging lifelong friendships with peers committed to CCD, but it has become the pipeline to our board and to other leadership opportunities within the association. As an extension of our core commitment to indigenous leadership development, we particularly focus on seeing leaders of color strongly represented in our cohort program, but not to the exclusion of our white brothers and sisters. Because of this initiative, CCDA is primed and ready to pass the leadership baton to a new generation of men and women. Why not take the bold step of applying for a cohort?

Community Based Advocacy

In the twenty-five-year history of CCDA, our efforts at biblical justice have been championed by lifetime board member Mary Nelson. In the last five years, CCDA has ventured into the deep waters of advocating for immigration reform, initially because of my passion for the issue but increasingly with the support of our entire board and the majority of our membership. Our approach to engaging in justice issues and advocacy is unique and is marked by our CCD philosophy.

In reality, ours is a community-based advocacy approach. For decades, our members have been involved in local justice issues in their communities and neighborhoods. On a national level, we are guided by this same principle: If a policy or system is hurting or oppressing our neighbors, we must raise our voices and confront those issues.

Presently, we are committed to pursuing advocacy and policy solutions related to three key issues: immigration, mass incarceration and education. We need your voice to assure that our neighbors who are affected by these critical issues can experience true justice.

Flourishing Neighborhoods Initiative

Fifty years ago, President Lyndon B. Johnson declared a "war on poverty," which set in motion a series of bills and acts creating programs such as Head Start, food stamps, work study, and Medicare and Medicaid. The programs initiated under Johnson brought about significant results, reducing rates of poverty and improving living standards for many of America's poor. Unfortunately, in many instances welfare programs targeted at the poor also created debilitating dependency instead of creating a lift out of poverty, which was the goal. In fact, the poverty rate has remained steady since the 1970s, and today Americans have allowed poverty to fall off the national agenda. Just think about how little we have heard about poverty in the last two presidential elections, where almost all of the focus was on the middle class and the wealthy.

While many would argue that empowering the "haves" should lead to the rising of the economic ship for everyone (including those on the margins of our economic system), the poor have been invisible in the national debate.

The church has struggled with putting those on the margins in the center of ministry and missional efforts. We have often gotten caught up in a spirit of growth and prosperity at the expense of prioritizing involvement with the poor.

Recently, President Obama established new "Promise Zones" in twenty major cities to help empower vulnerable neighborhoods by creating jobs, bettering education, improving housing and implementing other community-led efforts to create flourishing neighborhoods.

Maybe it is time for CCDA and the church to declare our own renewed commitment to address poverty in our nation and across the world. If you feel a burden for the vulnerable neighborhoods in your city, let's partner together to ensure that every neighborhood in our nation can flourish for the glory of God.

Regional Networks

The idea of seeing CCDA regional networks established has been on our drawing board for twenty-five years. Finally, we are ready to respond to the many requests from our members in every corner of the United States to establish official CCDA networks. Our hope is that these networks will be driven by local CCDA members who have a vision and a burden to see more effective CCD ministry become established in their cities and regions.

In the near future we envision a local network in your region that will offer you and your ministry support, training and inspiration as you implement the work of CCD in a vulnerable neighborhood. Be on the lookout for a local CCDA network near you and get plugged in.

National Office

The biggest privilege I have as the CEO of CCDA is working alongside a fantastic team. I could not be more enthused about every one of our staff. They are ready and eager to serve our members. Visit our website at www.ccda.org or give us a call at our headquarters in Chicago, but remember, we are not CCDA—you are!

APPENDIX 2

A History of National Conferences of the CCDA

1989
Held in Chicago, Illinois
Plenary talks by John Perkins, Bob Lupton and Wayne Gordon
Attendance: 140

1990
Held in Chicago, Illinois
Keynote speakers included Tom Skinner, Hamon Cross, John Perkins, Mary Nelson, Glen Kehrein, Wayne Gordon, Dolphus Weary and Bob Lupton
Attendance: 350

1991
Held in Atlanta, Georgia
Theme: Expanding the Dream, Restoring Community
Attendance: 400

1992
Held in Detroit, Michigan
Theme: Restoring Community, Building Community
Attendance: 800

1993
Held in Jackson, Mississippi
Theme: Looking Back, Moving Forward
Attendance: 1,000

1994
Held in Baltimore, Maryland
Theme: Combining Faith and Works—Rebuilding Our Communities Together
Attendance: 1,200

1995
Held in Denver, Colorado
Theme: For Such a Time As This—Christian Community Development
Attendance: 1,500

1996
Held in Pittsburgh, Pennsylvania
Theme: Rivers of Justice, Bridges of Mercy
Attendance: 1,900

1997
Held in Birmingham, Alabama
Theme: Revolution, Reconciliation and Revival
Attendance: 2,000

1998
Held in St. Louis, Missouri
Theme: Integrity, Vulnerability, Brokenness
Attendance: 2,200

1999 (Tenth Anniversary)
Held in Chicago, Illinois
Theme: Renewing People for a New Millennium
Attendance: 3,500

2000
Held in New York, New York
Theme: Stay Connected Through Prayer, Technology, Reconciliation and Justice
Attendance: 1,300

2001
Held in Dallas, Texas
Theme: Come Together: Tradition to Transition to Transformation
Attendance: 1,600

2002
Held in Pasadena, California
Theme: What Are We Going to Do About It? Healthcare, Racism, Housing, Criminal Justice System, Education, Materialism, Youth, Homelessness
Attendance: 1,800

2003
Held in New Orleans, Louisiana
Theme: New Wineskins for Our Changing Communities
Attendance: 1,900

2004
Held in Atlanta, Georgia
Theme: Living The Kingdom Now: Restoring Communities in the Name of Christ
Attendance: 2,000

2005
Held in Indianapolis, Indiana
Theme: Taking It Back: Radical Redemption of Our Communities
Attendance: 2,200

2006
Held in Philadelphia, Pennsylvania
Theme: Cities of Love with Liberty and Justice for All
Attendance: 2,200

2007
Held in St. Louis, Missouri
Theme: Show Me Jesus Beyond These Walls
Attendance: 2,400

2008
Held in Miami, Florida
Theme: Seeking the Peace of the City— Shalom
Attendance: 2,000

2009
Held in Cincinnati, Ohio
Theme: Pursuing Kingdom Priorities
Attendance: 2,500

2010 (Twenty-Year Anniversary Celebration)
Held in Chicago, Illinois
Theme: Remember the Past, Rejoice in the Present, Reimagine the Future
Attendance: 3,200

2011
Held in Indianapolis, Indiana
Theme: Innovate
Attendance: 2,300

2012
Held in Minneapolis, Minnesota
Theme: Reconcile
Attendance: 2,600

2013
Held in New Orleans, Louisiana
Theme: Cultivate
Attendance (est.): 2,700

NOTES

[1]Ron Sider, *Rich Christians in an Age of Hunger* (Downers Grove, IL: InterVarsity Press, 1977); John Perkins, *Let Justice Roll Down* (Ventura, CA: Gospel Light, 1976).

[2]Spencer Perkins and Chris Rice, *Sake of the Gospel* (Downers Grove, IL: InterVarsity Press, 1993).

[3]Bob Lupton, in *Restoring At-Risk Communities,* ed. John Perkins (Grand Rapids: Baker, 1995), pp. 81-82.

[4]Maia Szalavitz, "Study: Whites More Likely to Abuse Drugs Than Blacks," *Time,* November 7, 2001, http://healthland.time.com/2011/11/07/study-whites-more-likely-to-abuse-drugs-than-blacks/; Human Rights Watch, "Decades of Disparity: Drug Arrests and Race in the United States," 2009, www.hrw.org/sites/default/files/reports/us0309web_1.pdf.

[5]Glen Kehrein, "The Local Church and Christian Community Development," in *Restoring At-Risk Communities,* ed. John Perkins (Grand Rapids: Baker, 1995), pp. 176-77.

[6]Ibid.

[7]Mark Sheerin, "Why I Left World Vision for Finance," *Christianity Today,* February 22, 2013, www.christianitytoday.com/thisisourcity/7thcity/why-i-left-world-vision-for-finance.html.

[8]Bob Lupton, *Return Flight* (Atlanta: FCS Urban Ministries, 1993), n.p.

[9]Reggie McNeal, foreword to Eric Swanson and Sam Williams, *To Transform a City* (Grand Rapids: Zondervan, 2010), p. 12.

[10]Swanson and Williams, *To Transform a City,* n.p.

[11]Martin Luther King Jr., *A Testament of Hope* (New York: HarperCollins, 2003), p. 578.

CONTRIBUTORS

Joe Atkins is associate pastor of Lawndale Community Church and cofounder and director of Hope House Ministry. He lives in Chicago, Illinois.

Jonathan Brooks is senior pastor of Canaan Community Church and CEO of Canaan Community Redevelopment Corporation. He lives in Chicago, Illinois.

Christine Brooks Nolf is the executive director and cofounder of Mica Community Development. She lives in Costa Mesa, California.

Noel Castellanos is the CEO of the Christian Community Development Association. He lives in Chicago, Illinois.

Sami DiPasquale is the executive director of Ciudad Nueva Community Outreach. He lives in a low-income community on the US–Mexico border.

Bethany Dudley is the church and community consultant for Communities First Association, and the education and curriculum director for the Christian Community Development Association. She lives in Chicago, Illinois.

Scott Lundeen is associate director of programs for Urban Impact Ministries. He lives in Denver, Colorado.

Bob Lupton is founder and president (emeritus) of FCS Urban Ministries. He lives in Atlanta, Georgia.

Bruce Miller is CEO of Lawndale Christian Health Center. He lives in Chicago, Illinois.

"Q" Nellum is a teacher/mentor in Denver public schools and the founder of Arts N' the Hood. She lives in Denver, Colorado.

Jared Onserio is CEO of Christian Community Development of Africa. He lives in Kibera, Kenya.

Patty Prasada-Rao is the chief operating officer of the Christian Community Development Association. She lives in Chicago, Illinois.

Jember Teferra is the director of Integrated Holistic Approach Urban Development Project. She lives in Addis Ababa, Ethiopia.

Ryan Ver Wys is the executive director of Kingdom Causes Bellflower. He lives in Bellflower, California.

Thurman Williams is senior pastor of New Song Community Church. He lives in Baltimore, Maryland.